Naked Wednesdays

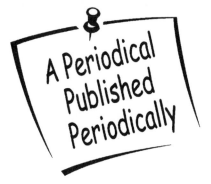

A Periodical
Published
Periodically

Ina Christensen, Phil Hahn,

Sandy Kretzschmar,

Angela Lebakken, Faye Newman

and Betty Wetzel

ISBN: 0-937861-68-5
First Printing December 2005

The Naked Wednesdays Writers Group

WEGFERDS' PRINTING & PUBLICATIONS
North Bend, OR 97459

Printed in the U.S.A.

DEDICATION

This publication is gratefully dedicated
to our hostess, supporter, and friend,
Trish Hermann of Books By The Bay,
for generously giving six ripening rowdies
a private place to commit the mischief
that created this book.
Bless you, Trish, and as they say,
thanks for the use of the hall.

THE NAKED WEDNESDAYS
WRITERS GROUP

NAKED WEDNESDAYS
Table of Contents

NAKED WEDNESDAYS

Betty Wetzel

T*his must be how an early Christian mother feels when pushed into the arena filled with wild beasts. The lions will descend and tear my baby to bits.* As the group reviewed my literary masterpiece, visions of it being eviscerated, with the bits and pieces torn to shreds and digested, filled my over-vivid imagination. Prepared for the worst, I finally heard, through my fears, words of encouragement:

"Excellent detail."

"This gives a great picture."

"What a treasure."

Basking in this praise, I was immunized, almost, against the critique and suggestions for changes that followed. Surprised, I found my baby not only alive and well at the end of the session, but improved in content and readability. A more interesting presentation for future readers.

Over the three years our writers' group has been together, we have met faithfully every Wednesday afternoon. None of the six misses a meeting unless absolutely necessary. Each of us respects and honors the creative process. We laugh together and sometimes cry together, fostering mutual respect and trust of one another's viewpoint. We take critiquing seriously and our work is all the better for it.

Into the Lion's Den? Terrifying, yes. But I wouldn't miss it for the world!

Nice, France

*The following excerpt is taken from **The Emperor's Daughter**, Sandy Kretzschmar's astonishing adventures as she uncovers a life as Julia, the exiled daughter of Augustus Caesar.*

GETTING BY IN FRANCE
Sandy Kretzschmar

All the way to the French border the train shimmied like a Moroccan dancer. I tried sleeping but couldn't. The previous night in Ventimiglia, bells from the Romanesque church across from my *pensione* bonged out of tune. Every thirty minutes the window rattled, the bed vibrated. Somehow I'd managed to sleep through the three a.m. fortissimo tolling.

Once in France, the rhythmic clack-clacking of smoother tracks lulled me into drowsiness; even the scenery tempted me to sleep. My tired eyes closed. Too bad my letter to Monsieur Henri Rolland had been returned. How would I find him now? He was my hope for locating Julia's marble likeness. Maybe when I'd called from home, the tourist office had given me the wrong address or misunderstood. And if I found Henri, how would I dare present myself? How would I tell a renowned archeologist and former member of the French Resistance I was Caesar's daughter? Would he believe me? Would he see Julia in me? For months I'd practiced what I'd say, hoping he'd understand, working out every possible scenario in my head. I nodded off dreaming of Henri...

...ushered on rays from a golden sunset, I arrived at the French country chapel turned museum. Outside, an old man slumped on a stone bench beneath an olive tree. Behind him the oak door stood ajar. The air seemed drenched in lavender dust and ripening olives. Accepting my six francs with a guttural groan, he waved his serpentine cane for me to pass, and watched with curiosity as I first hesitated then crossed the threshold. Inside, amber sunbeams filtered through tiny windows. Light seemed to come from all angles, illuminating a marble bust at center floor. She balanced on a tall pedestal, her face away from me. Shadows crossed in angles that fooled the eye into believing a marble head could levitate. I hesitated. What if she disappointed me? What if she wasn't beautiful? Why did I need her to be beautiful? Would seeing my face from the past send me into shock just as the first time I saw Augustus Caesar's lifelike statue? I tiptoed nearer, expectant, fearful yet hopeful, comforted now by a blush on her cheek from the last rays of sunset. Her details blurred. I reached to touch her crystalline lips.

The old man cleared his throat and rose from his bench. Ambling toward me through the entrance and into dusty shadows, he pointed his cane and grumbled in a Provençal dialect. I stepped back expecting a blow from his staff, but he sighed and wobbled beside me before turning to face the bust of Julia. As afternoon light dissolved, he spoke in murmuring tones, displaying a devotion bordering on love, of what must have been the remarkable story of her discovery... .

A shriek from the train whistle jolted me. I couldn't afford to fall asleep, miss my stop and wind up in the Pyrenees. I moved to the aisle and leaned out the open window, watching the train trace the shoreline. Salt mist kissed my face. Bright morning light transformed the Mediterranean Sea into effervescent sparkles. Peace engulfed me. The enchanted landscape rolled by in a constant sequence of scenes, like watching someone else's travel video. This was the land of Chagall and Matisse, yet somehow it surprised me that the perfumed landscape carried the same vibrant shades as my textbook's reproductions of their paintings.

Through one enticing town after another, I yearned to leap from the train and surrender to nature where the sea lapped onto the tiny beaches of *Cote d' Azur*. I'd been here before, many times. No doubt about it. I'd always loved this coastline. I knew in the sense that no one had ever told me, in the sense that one learns to trust one's instincts, that the region we now call France had been my home in five lifetimes, including Julia's travels here with Marcus Agrippa.

France. So strange and yet so familiar. Fear of French vowels made my limited sing-song Italian feel like a welcome comfort zone. I'd listened to "Getting By In French" tapes until total confusion clogged my brain. Italian wasn't so intimidating once I'd learned to manage the lira and understand numbers that were rattled off at light speed by shopkeepers and hoteliers. Aligning with my quest meant acting as if I'd left all fear behind. Hopefully, France would not be a traumatic experience.

Memories of Georgia's plea ("Oh Julia, Julia, Julia!") carried the same cadence as the slowing train. How fitting that my marble portrait had been lost until this lifetime. Where would I find her, my Roman face?

At exactly high noon, ten minutes after arriving in

Nice, I entered the tourist assist office, beside the train station. A plaque on the door said due to remodeling, the Musèe Marc Chagall was closed for the year, the Musèe Matisse for two more weeks. Again, my timing was off. During my last phone call home, when I'd whined that all the impressionist art was unavailable, my husband had chided, "You're not there for the Van Goghs. That's another trip."

A striking woman seated at the desk raised her alert brown eyes and regarded me with hauteur. Spiked bronze-colored hair crowned her sharp-featured face. I swallowed momentary fear, realizing I faced a descendent of the Amazon warrior-priestesses who had fled to southern France. It is said they resembled horses. Like a living artifact, she stared back, down her long equine nose, ready to make karmic amends via the tourist office for the Amazon tradition of routinely murdering strangers.

I asked how I might locate Henri Rolland, archeologist. She made three phone calls while I paced anxiously, scanning printed French words on wall posters, brochures and a magazine rack. One publication, *Les Dossiers D'Archeologie,* had a cover photo of ancient columns surrounding the dry pit of a former Roman thermal bath. I lifted the magazine and flipped past articles on pottery, wall frescoes and floor mosaics. Among the back pages, one black-and-white photo, slightly out of focus, showed a bald man with a moustache. He held a larger-than-life-size marble head of a woman against his striped suit. Her moon-shaped face had a bashed nose and marcel waves reminiscent of the nineteen twenties. The caption read:

"HENRI ROLLAND LE 'DECOUVREUR' DE GLANUM."

Henri, as close as my fingertips! The magazine date read *JUILLET-AOUT*, July — August, six months previous. The head he held in the photo looked familiar, but it didn't quite seem like Julia, at least from what I recalled of the Norwegian author's description. The shape was too round, and Elisabeth Dored never mentioned Julia's marble head as having a broken nose. But she had seen it in 1959, thirty-one years ago.

My heart quickened. Soon, with luck and the gods willing, I would meet with Henri. If necessary, I'd locate a translator. We'd share stories. He'd usher me through the museum and proudly present Julia. Maybe he'd believe... .

The Amazon cleared her throat.

I turned.

"Monsieur Rolland is dead."

"Dead? He can't be dead!" I waved the archeology digest like a pennant. My voice issued the same shrieking tone I'd screamed while fighting off Rome's rapacious Gypsies.

The Amazon flinched and covered the receiver with her hand. "How could he do that?" I yelled again. "I've waited a whole year to meet him!"

Two travelers with red Canadian maple-leaf flags on their coats looked on, wide-eyed. She acknowledged them with a raised brow.

I felt ashamed. The self-centeredness of Julia, Caesar's spoiled only child, had crept through again, showing up when I most needed to make a good impression.

The Amazon resumed her stiff air of propriety, turned her steady warrior-priestess gaze on me, and in an accent as divine as French pastry said, "We all have to go sometime."

COMING OF AGE WITH THE MONKEY WARDS CATALOGUE

Phil Hahn

I suspect it's become almost impossible these days for a boy to reach puberty without having acquired at least a journeyman's knowledge of the female body. After all, pictures of naked ladies abound in magazines from *Playboy* to *Vogue*, and hardly any movie worth its salt reaches the final fadeout without at least a fleeting glimpse of a starlet in her birthday suit. And if all else fails, the modern boy can always tune in an adult film on cable TV and find out more about the female anatomy than he cares to know.

In my day, of course, things were different. My primary source of such information was the *Lingerie* section of the Montgomery Ward mail-order catalogue. Everybody called it *Monkey Wards* then, for some reason. I'm sorry I don't know why, but I don't.

Anyway, whenever my pre-pubescent curiosity got the better of me, I'd wait until I was alone in the house, and furtively haul out the trusty catalogue.

You could start with either *Brassieres* or *Briefs*, depending upon your whim, but you couldn't look at both at the same time. In those days, you see, they didn't show a whole girl all at once. Not in her underwear, they didn't. They showed either a girl from the waist up, wearing a bra, or a girl from the waist down, wearing underpants. But never, ever, an entire girl, full length, wearing both bra *and* underpants. I don't know the

"HE LEARNED ABOUT WOMEN FROM HER"

reason for *this*, either.

What I *do* know is that these half-girl photos led to some unfortunate misconceptions. Some of us came to the conclusion that girls come in sections, like stovepipe, and have to be assembled. This, as you probably know by now, is erroneous. It was a widespread belief in those days, however, and I'm sad to report that some of us still have our suspicions.

Adding to the confusion was the fact that you could turn to the *Foundation Garments* section and see an entire female, top and bottom together, decked out in a sturdy corset and a serious-looking brassiere. These women, however, were invariably more mature and of greater girth, giving rise to the theory that as girls get older and fatter, they grow together and become one-unit items at last.

Misconceptions or no, the good old Monkey Wards catalogue gave me a hint of future delights without overheating my tender sensibilities, and I shall be forever grateful. It is my firm belief that if the *Lingerie* section had shown me less, I might have gone on to some form of socially unacceptable behavior, like window-peeping, and ended up in a life of crime. On the other hand, if it had shown me any more, it might have diluted the thrill of discovery on that wonderful day when the real thing came along.

I'm not saying they're doing it wrong these days, mind you. I believe that education is always beneficial, and young boys today probably have a much better shot at handling sex in a mature manner than any of us catalogue kids ever did.

Still, I can't help thinking that those of us raised with the Monkey Wards system were a little gentler, a little more chivalrous and quite a bit nicer to the girls than young men are today.

But that's to be expected. After all, you tend to handle a lady with a lot more care when you're secretly worried she might break in half.

*Excerpted from **Carly's Eyes**, a novel in progress. Whitney McCaine and her seven-year-old daughter, Lissy, have taken a day off to ride their horses, Spirit and Jahai, on the beach.*

FLY AWAY FAIR

Faye Newman

> *What delight to back the flying steed that challenges the wind*
> *for speed! — seems native more of air than earth!*
> James Sheridan Knowles

Wind whipped through Whitney's hair, drying the sheen of perspiration to a mask on her neck and face. Ahead of her, Spirit's gorgeous copper tail flew, sweeping behind him, a half-mast banner displaying masculine power and pride. Lissy's slim buttocks gave no hint of yesterday's superglue; she bounced in the saddle as if attached to a spring and her squeals of delight could be heard for miles along the semi-deserted beach.

Cool winter sunshine glinted off the choppy surface of the sea between pockets of fog, and the nippy air pinked their cheeks, but they were warm enough in light jackets and jeans. Their shouts and laughter were swallowed by the ocean's roar. Waves curled and crashed ashore, then rolled gently up the beach to tease their horses' hoofs.

Here and there, a beachcomber gave Lissy an amused laugh, but for the most part, Whitney and her daughter had miles of dark, wet sand and frothy surf to themselves. And Lissy was making the most of it.

Whitney caught her breath when Spirit scraped a toe as if to stumble in the sand. But in the past eight weeks, Spirit and Lissy had become a team, part and parcel of one another, a singular flow of motion, whether fast or slow. Now, Lissy's small muscular back undulated with each stretch of the gelding's front legs, urging him on, faster, ever faster. And still the little Arabian delivered, his mouth open as if laughing along with his rider, his joyful whinny echoing against the foredune and the islands of Douglas firs.

Jahai, carrying a heavier load, kept up, but doing so required all of his speed and conditioning. Spirit was fast and agile.

Whitney forgot her troubles, exulted in the ride, laughed with it, and bounced in her own saddle, scarcely feeling a twinge from her summer injury. Jahai, doing what he loved to do above all else — running — screamed with as much joy and delight as Lissy. Ahead, a pair of stacked driftwood trees, carried in by some past storm, loomed in Lissy's path. They seemed to have floated out of a low-lying patch of fog like ghostly figures entwined in passion, fading in, fading out. Whitney's heart did a rapid, end-over-end tumble, but Spirit didn't miss a step. Western saddle or no, Lissy leaned far over the horn. Clutching her horse's mane, she supported his jump with her body. The pair sailed up, up, and away, a graceful fantasy figure with a rider, clearing an imaginary moon rendered invisible in the fog by the sun hanging above the dunes, burning away treacherous mists.

Mists that concealed dangers from unsuspecting children and helpless mothers.

THROUGH TIME AND SPACE

Angela Lebakken

*"You can't go home again.
You can't recover the past."*
Thomas Wolfe

This typical September day is anything but typical for me. My brother, his wife and I board the Empire Builder to journey from Portland, Oregon to Fargo, North Dakota. We are going back home and I smile with pleasure as I picture the familiar streets and the cottage where I grew up. Even the name Empire Builder stirs memories of me as a frightened teenager taking this train from Chicago to home. Heading in the opposite direction with the same destination will be a first and I resolve to pay close attention to the landscape we'll travel through. When I hear the final ALL ABOARD and feel the chug as we start to move out of the station I settle in my seat prepared to stare out the window; to soak in the beauty as it passes me by.

Ah — the Columbia River Gorge — clouds float in multi-layered splendor and the setting sun parts the billows majestically as if God Himself would suddenly appear. Look — a double rainbow stretched across the sky... .

After a night reclined in my roomy seat, wrapped snugly in the blanket I've toted along, I awaken to a sunrise that blushes the vapors pink like the cheeks of a happy toddler. Swaying, grabbing the backs of seats, I wamble my way to the observation car and a cup of steaming coffee. From this vantage point I can often see both the engine and the caboose as we wend our way through Glacier National Park with its rushing streams and waterfalls and snow-capped mountain peaks. A herd of antelope run in the distance. At play?

Mellowed now by the rhythmic clacking of the wheels and endless scenic charm before me, I relax and sip my coffee.

Arriving in Havre, pronounced 'have her' — you can imagine the story — we climb down and stretch our legs, breathing in the hint of winter in the crisp, autumn air. Never venturing far, for we have been warned the train will leave with or without us. Coming into the plains you may think you are in for a boring day. Surprise! See the black and brown cattle grazing behind fence posts that lean every which way. Hear the swoosh as thousands of birds lift from small ponds. Sigh with the weathered barn as it sinks to its knees in supplication. Horses – black, brown, white and spotted — rest on the rolling hills.

The train whistles us through time and space. Picturesque little settlements tempt me to uproot and move, but I remember the harsh winters and say "no thank you." Fields of sunflowers with heads bowed wait for harvest. Oops — a junkyard of abandoned cars — we pause to pray for our planet. Oil wells here and there nod to us as we approach. Tree limbs are buffeted by the ever-present wind that howls across flatlands with nothing to subdue it. Clouds in varying shades of gray hang low and thick as we, secure and warm in our seats, idle the day watching the world go by.

The train pulls into the Fargo station on time to the minute (2:10 AM) and my brother, his wife and I step down to plant our feet once again on native soil. Our destination is Wahpeton — the name a contraction of the Native American word Warpeotonwe, meaning Leaf Village. Wahpeton where we find we *can* go home again but we experience deja vu with a spin.

The spin starts on the 50 mile drive south from Fargo. I insist on taking the "Minnesota side," my memory certain this highway curves along the meandering Red River. It doesn't. We never see the river. Until we come into Breckrenridge, Wahpeton's counterpart across the state divide. People, waiting for a parade to start, line the streets of this city of 4,000. "Imagine that. A welcome home parade for us," I say with a grin. How did they know? Alas, it is Headwaters Day, something I'd never seen celebrated when I was growing up. The twenty-first annual celebration in recognition of the confluence of two small rivers, the Bois de Sioux and the Ottertail, to form the mighty Red River of the North.

After checking into a motel we set out to explore our hometown. The small community has grown and yet shrunk, too. Streets now number all the way to twenty-two, but such short blocks they are. We figure out where the gardens had been. Daddy's vegetable patches, outside the city limits, where we plucked potato bugs and hauled produce home on our bikes, up a hill so steep we huffed. Where was that hill now? Had it been leveled?

Our visit to St. John's Catholic Church, on Main Street, inspires an awestruck wonder and we look at each other with questioning eyes. The three massive front doors have been replaced by ornate stained-glass windows. What was the altar is now the entrance. My mind spins in eerie confusion.

I feel disoriented — as if my childhood had done a 180 degree flip. As if church and Catholic and nuns and ...and *everything* were never what they had seemed to be. So much different and yet with a hint of sameness as if the curtain had dropped on Act One and lifted again for Act Two.

With a sense of loss, I climb back into the rental car,

ready to search for a landmark — any landmark that will reassure me my childhood memories have some validity. We head for home.

When we arrive at what was 518 Sixth Street North, we stand in wide-eyed disbelief. A space — a pitifully small space — is all that marks the spot. Green, gently rolling lawns, a white picket fence surrounding a flower garden, a tire swinging from a rope in the big tree. Standing here, feeling boxed in by the two large white houses, I have an urge to push them apart with my elbows. To open up the pinched, inadequate space that had once held my home. I always knew it was a small house, even when I was little in it, but certainly not this small. Gone, as if vanished into thin air, and the other houses growing and spreading to fill the void. I stammer in my desperation to recount what once was. There should at least be a plaque acknowledging my parents who laughed and cried, grew old and died here. A plaque listing the five children who found safety and themselves in the shelter of a tiny home that is no more.

I long to return to my present life. I imagine the hypnotic train ride and the soothing whistle in the night, like a lullaby, easing my mind as I ponder which memories to celebrate and which to bid adieu.

*This is an excerpt from **A White Stone**, a coming of age memoir. The 67,750 word manuscript is in its final editing.*

CHOCOLATE DROPS AND BABY CRIES

Ina Christensen

It's Christmas and we have a tree. I clap my hands I'm so happy. It's a small scraggly sort of tree, but I think it's beautiful. I'm glad Mama hasn't forgotten that it's Christmas. I never know with Mama. One year, she'll celebrate a holiday, and the next year forgets all about it.

We don't hang stockings, but Dad comes home with brand new drinking cups. He says the cups will work just fine instead of stockings. We always drink from tin cups because there's so many kids in our family, and glass cups are always breaking and need to be replaced. The new cups are so shiny I can see my face, and when Dad fastens them to our tree they look pretty. Best of all, he puts a cup on for each of us, so that we don't have to share.

I hope the pretty tree will make Mama smile. Ever since we buried the baby last September, Mama has been real quiet and sad. All of us are careful not to mention the baby, though sometimes Mama does. I heard her tell Dad that, if the baby had lived, she would have named her Stella. I think Stella is a pretty name. Much prettier than Ina or Ida. I'm named after a dead grandmother, and Ida is named after a dead aunt. I wonder if maybe Mama has run out of dead relatives.

Christmas morning, Mama comes out of her

bedroom carrying a brightly wrapped package for each of us. She says Nita has sent them all the way from Oregon. Mama has had them put away, so we could open them on Christmas day. In our new tin cups are three pieces of chocolate candy, the kind of candy that is shaped like little hills and has different colored centers. I bite into one of mine, careful to take tiny bites so it will last longer. The chocolate melts and makes my tongue tingle with sweetness and I know this is my lucky day. The center is pink; my very favorite kind.

It's been a happy day; even Dad is home instead of out drinking with his cronies. Mama fixes us a nice supper. Afterwards, we all move into the living room so we can listen to the radio. Dad fiddles with the knob until he finds a station. He is the only one allowed to mess with the radio, so we listen to what he likes. Finally, he finds a program and sits down in his chair. We can hear people laughing and talking, Mama says that's because it has a live audience. The singing and music are beautiful. Then, about halfway through the program, we hear a baby cry. Mama's face crumples up and the tears start falling, as she rushes from the room.

I know then, this is the end of our happy day.

JUST BROWSING, THANK YOU

Phil Hahn

"Used Romance," the bookshelf said,
A status up with which I'm fed.
I'd like a new one, shiny, bright
To crawl in bed with me tonight.
But I suppose I'd be confused
By romance that wasn't used,
So I will tightly zip my pants
And just make do with used romance.

RETURNING HOME

Ina Christensen

I was born of light when the stars were new.
Within the mists I walked with my creator,
 happy, content... and then...
My spirit gathered, stretched, yearned, dreamed,
 to be more...
I snuggled my quiver of tools, wrapped firmly in
 magic and make-believe, and left.
Up the ragged mountains I climbed, nameless
 nothing surrounded me.
I lingered there, seeking shelter among the
 shadows.
I became afraid, so I sought counsel from the world.
I chose to cleave to ideas and beliefs not my own.
To sing someone else's song.
But, I learned, and eventually...
I remembered.
I was born of light when the stars were new.

REINCARNATION

Sandy Kretzschmar

In 1942...
I was only a boy
French, Jewish
And the last target
In town
When that laughing Nazi
Shot me.

He could still be alive.
But it's all right. I forgave him
Ten years ago. I like my life,
Who I am now.

Except I can't speak French
Or read Hebrew.
And I don't know where
My family is.

Original watercolor by Vanessa Jorgenson

I AM A WAVE: A MEDITATION

Faye Newman

I am a wave.
I rise and fall, pulled by forces of Luna
Tugged by the power of Terra.
My cells intermingle with water beside me,
Beneath me, before, behind and within me.
I swirl, expanding here, contracting there.
I am a wave, alive and free.
My hair floats, each tress a screen for a fish,
A bit of foam.
I twist and turn, stretch and bend, spread my arms,
Dance on my toes, roll and unfold.
Froth racing over sand.
I am a wave.
Light as air, free and unbound.
I am a wave.
Warmed by the sun,
I stretch to meet its shimmering rays
I am a ray.
Soaring from the depths
Hands together, arms before me,
I wing toward the sun.
I am a ray.
I ascend, a wave becoming a ray.
My droplets sift fine and soft as fluff, a wisp of a mist.

Together, we are a cloud.
Guided and propelled by the wind,
We sigh over sea and sand
And toy with snow-capped peaks.
I am a cloud.
I sail over mountains to the valley,
Warmed by the light,
Darkening, softly, I fall and moisten the earth.
I am rain.
Absorbed by the earth, drawn into a root,
Up to a stem, and to the tips of each leaf.
I am earth, I am rain, I am a wave,
I am a ray, I am a cloud.
I am all of everything.
Joining with the sun, I am kissed by the wind,
And a flower is born.
I am a petal.
Day is done, Luna beckons. I fall to earth.
My cells disperse, each one light as breath.
I am earth.
I nourish a plant.
Waves fall and I am drawn deep, deep into soil,
Carried in droplets,
Dancing through earth. I run, gurgling,
Pouring forth, a stream washing down the valley
And back, back to the sea.
I am a wave. I expand and contract.
I roll and unfold.
I am a wave.

HAIKU
Ina Christensen

The Critique Group
En garde, pencils fly
Naked Wednesday Afternoon
Dull prose to sharpen.

The Party
Scarlet tinged sunset
Raptors in a flooded field
Two eagles frolic.

COQUILLE FALLS

Angela Lebakken
Original watercolor by *Vanessa Jorgensen*

Sunlight, like a spotlight, highlights the tree.
We stop, Vanessa, Betty and me,
And we stare at this Face that we see.
She isn't afraid and neither are we.

She gently mouths "Oh,"
As if she wants us to know
She'll be watching. As we walk away
"Oh," becomes the word for the day.

"Oh," when I stumble.
"Oh," when you slide.
"Oh," when we see the iris 'long side.

"Oh, oh, oh," when the falls first appear.
The tumble and rush is the music we hear.
Oooh," and "oh" as delighted we sit
Proud of ourselves and feeling so fit.

Happy to help when steps are too steep
For Betty's short legs to make the big leap.
Laughter, camaraderie, tickled with joy
Not a care in the world, "oh, oh, oh boy."

Huffing and puffing, more sturdy on feet
But pushing my heart, beat after beat.
Once more, here we are — the face in the tree.
To remain in the sun, she's turned a degree.

"Oh," she says and we "Oh" in return
Glad for the beauty, glad for the burn.
At last to the start and our car and our seats.
At last to our rest and good-bye to retreats.

*The following excerpt is taken from **The Emperor's Daughter**, a book in progress by Sandy Kretzschmar.*

INTO THE MOUTH OF THE WOLF

Sandy Kretzschmar

He who loves should live,
he who knows not how to love should die,
and he who obstructs love should die twice.
— Graffiti on the house of Lucius Caecilius Jucundus, Pompeii

The next morning, I phoned home from the *pensione* lobby and told my husband, Ruben, how magical last night had been — bells tolling in the distance and the Coliseum dominating the black Roman sky while the moon disappeared into an eerie burnt red eclipse. And how three women I'd met only two days before had extended their time in Rome to help me free a thousand spirits trapped in a vortex. Now that task was done. Time to play. I let Ruben know today's destination was Pompeii via Naples. Annie and I would be meeting the Australian sisters at the train station. I'd have to find out how to get my Eurail pass validated. Then Annie and I would part. She'd take the train to Florence and I'd go with Saucy and Mica to Pompeii. I reassured him, saying the sisters were diligent chaperons even if they were only twenty and twenty-one. I didn't mention the wacky Aussies could most likely get me into a world of trouble. Later, I learned Ruben misunderstood, telling everyone, "Sandy's perfectly safe now. She's traveling with sisters. You know, with nuns."

After hanging up the phone, I asked the *pensione* owner

if he would store my baggage overnight. He frowned through thin, chapped lips, shaking his head. So rather than haul forty pounds of luggage on an overnight trip I rented an entire room for two bags. After the hotel breakfast of a hard brioche and orange juice, I put extra honey and marmalade packets into my coat pocket for Saucy and Mica and strapped on my backpack. Then I helped Annie carry a desk-size steamer trunk down two flights of stairs to the street. She said we didn't need to call a taxi. The station was near enough. Annie led the way to the train station, pulling the khaki trunk by its leather strap. My job was to lift the trunk's rickety back end onto curbs and help her carry it across cobblestones so the dented wheels wouldn't fall off.

Under a clear cobalt sky, only rooftops warmed in the low February sun. Tall palazzos basked in Helios's radiance, soaking up heat and light and leaving the dim street in damp tones of winter melancholy. Our path was like a deep crevasse where a cold wind blew, chilling my face and hands. I craved one of those colorful wool scarves every Roman wore, even the men. For now I made do with the thin black shawl I'd bought at home, the one I foolishly thought would help me pass for Italian.

Annie set a brisk pace along purple sidewalk shadows, intent on catching her train to Florence. She pointed out the soot-stained police station as a landmark for finding my way back to the *pensione* of the hateful innkeepers. I didn't have a chance to pay attention to our route. The clackety-clacking trunk kept wobbling onto its side, almost falling into gutters. Every other block a wheel came lose and we had to stop and set it right, hoping it hadn't fallen into the maze of squashed chewing gum everywhere, or Rome's other sidewalk attraction....

Yuk!" I said, "There's enough spit on these sidewalks to permanently grease them."

Mia, Savoy and Annie in Rome

"Ha!" Annie laughed. "You should see Istanbul."

I wondered how I'd say goodbye to her, my new dear friend of two days. I'd have to survive on my own. Annie noted we had only thirty minutes to catch our trains and quickened her pace. After ten blocks of dodging garbage we came to a wide intersection. I still wasn't accustomed to Annie's style of jaywalking through moving traffic — that cavalier torrent of fearless Italians. My tour book had joked about the two types of pedestrians in Rome: the quick and the dead. We lifted the awkward trunk by its corners. She stepped purposefully off the curb and glared at oncoming motorists, the weighty trunk connecting us. I knew by now she'd neither hesitate nor run, but would keep a steady gait across lopsided lava street tiles until we reached the far sidewalk.

Midway in the busy street, blinding sunlight stabbed at my eyes. Reflected glare shot off passing cars that whizzed around us like a swarm of bees. I needed to shield my eyes from the sun, but I couldn't let go of the trunk. The rush of noxious air forced my hair into my eyes. I squinted. Beyond a double row of orange buses I thought I glimpsed the *Statzione Termini.*

"Annie, is that the station?"

Apparently, she didn't hear over the din of traffic. When we reached the opposite sidewalk we set the trunk down. Annie took off again, pulling it at an ever faster tempo. Before I could straighten, my coat jerked backward; the front zipper cut jagged teeth into my neck. I turned. A pygmy-size falcon-eyed woman hung onto my coat with one hand while concealing a child under a blanket.

I yelled and spun around, trying to fling her off. She clawed onto my backpack. Her kid had a grip on my pocket, small hands visible from beneath the blanket. I swatted at the bird-like woman. She wailed in some bizarre dialect as if she were the prey and I the Gypsy. Another woman, arrayed in feathery drab flounces, latched onto my left sleeve. Together they hauled me back into the street, into the path of a Mercedes. I screamed, but my scream was deadened by the blare of a horn as the Mercedes swerved past.

The Gypsies refused to let go of my coat. Three days of pent-up frustration erupted. I pounded my fists into tiers of frayed kerchiefs. I'm not sure what I hit. One woman fell away, squalling and shrieking what I'm certain were curses. I punched again. Maybe I hit the child; I hoped not. The woman carrying him didn't even stagger. Beeping cars sped around us, avoiding our skirmish like we were lepers scratching each other's sores.

I yelled for Annie, but my voice couldn't compete with the inherent chaos of Rome.

Amidst the whirl of speeding Fiats, Volkswagens and vans, the two Gypsy women, one still holding the child, backed away with scurrilous grimaces. An onslaught of cars honked at me to get out of the road. Back on the sidewalk, I looked for Annie and spotted her a half block away. She faded into traffic, behind taxis and buses parked at the *Termini*.

I ran after her to the station. Inside, hundreds of voices echoed and intertwined with the far-off hollow sounds of trains coming and going on any of twenty-two tracks. Gray and black confusion enveloped me from *nazionale* and *stranero* cigarettes and wretched lighting. Spunky Annie and her wobbly trunk were nowhere in sight.

I'd studied my train book the night before, memorizing the jargon. Now it came in handy as I searched the schedule board, separating *arrivo* from *partenza* and finding *binari* numbers for Florence and Naples. Twelve minutes until both our trains left. Maybe she would locate her train then search for me in whatever time remained.

First I had to find the Eurail window. My ticket wasn't valid until an official stamped it with today's date. Then it was worth three weeks of unlimited travel in seventeen countries. At the moment I could hardly imagine venturing beyond Italy. I checked my pockets. My inside security pocket still held passport, wallet and train pass. But the troglodyte child had emptied my outside pocket of the honey and marmalade packets I'd saved for the sisters.

I hurried past the *tabacchi* shop and windows marked *PRENOTAZIONE* — reservations, and *CAMBIO* — change, past huge corridors, the post office and unsavory aspects of humanity, back to the front of the station where I had entered. There I lost five minutes waiting in a long line at the Eurail window before a swarthy man stamped my ticket. Annie could be anywhere.

I found what I thought was the ticket line for Naples, in a wide corridor where six lines of people to six ticket windows squashed together. No one moved. No one spoke.

I joined them and waited. Five minutes passed. I turned to a middle-aged woman behind me. She was the first person of African descent I'd seen in Italy; maybe she spoke English. *"Scuzi,"* I said, "is this the line for Naples?" To my utter amazement the woman stared past my ear into space with the most determined muteness I've ever seen. She made no attempt to gesture, no eye contact, no vocalization, no apology. I tried again. *"Biglietti per Napoli?"* Tickets for Naples? Nothing. I searched faces of the dozen or so crowded within arm's reach; each individual avoided eye contact. I spoke to the man next to me with the same baffling result. I was completely invisible — except to thieves. I was beginning to hate Rome.

I left that stagnant line and searched again in a panic for Annie. The Italian saying, *into the mouth of the wolf,* was beginning to make sense. It means *good luck.*

I ran to another long corridor, the immense modern foyer, and realized I had been waiting and searching all that time in the wrong place. Precious time in the line to nowhere. Annie would now be on her train and there was nothing I could do but try to catch the train to Naples.

I darted across the foyer to the ticket booth and showed my Eurail pass to the clerk. *"Per fervore, Naploi,"* I said.

He noted the date with a blank expression and waived me through the turnstile. Across the concrete platform the Naples train moved forward. I raced to the *binario,* ran alongside, grabbed the hand rail and barely leaped into the rear door of the last car as the train picked up speed.

If I had to, I'd walk the entire length of the train until I found the sisters. Then I'd catch my breath. But they were in the next car. They saw me and bounced with glee, waving and calling my name.

Saucy insisted I take her seat in the crowded car while she stood. I had a first class ticket. I was not about to leave them just to go to the first class section. Before I could explain about getting lost and losing Annie, I was a rush of tears. "Damn," I said. "Can't one day pass here without my crying?"

"Annie must know you're okay," Mica said, reassuring me with a pat of her hand.

"I'm fine," I said, still shaken with adrenalin from the Gypsy attack and almost missing the train and the girls. Saucy noticed the cut at my throat. I explained how the Gypsy tugged on my coat; the zipper must have sliced me. "People here will lie and take advantage of you," Saucy said, as if she were twice my age, instead of the other way around. "You have to shape up if you're going to survive."

I knew she was right. Still, my spontaneous violence against the Gypsies embarrassed me. I'd fully intended to harm a malnourished human half my size. Three days in Rome had undone a decade of spiritual discipline. Now I understood what my husband had meant when he'd said he didn't want to come to Rome because he was afraid he'd kill someone.

The ride south from Rome felt surreal. I glimpsed remnants of Marcus Agrippa's aqueduct system standing in open fields, like battered sentinels, miles and miles of an arch here, a pile of rubble there, then a series of more arches. The train car swayed and shuddered from side to side. I needed the soothing motion. But every time I drifted off, I'd jump, startled by air molecules colliding in the whoosh of another train passing too near on adjacent tracks.

I leaned against the train's window and stared down at the blur of adjacent tracks and ties not wanting the girls to see how the landscape revived my tears. Blackberry vines, yucca and wildflowers grew alongside the tracks. We passed small-farm parcels with rustic houses, dark-green wooden shutters and big oak doors encased in crumbling, decomposing brick. Nothing but red-tile roofs. In some ways the scenes looked quite pastoral, in others like Italy still struggled to free itself from the poverty of the last war. The landscape had hardly changed in two thousand years. Long rows of short, gnarled grapevines formed crisscross patterns far into distant lavender hills. Old men, as bent and knotty as their vines, worked the dry and dusty rows pruning plants that must have been started in another century. The absence of towering trees bothered me. Only a few tall pines could be seen miles in the distance. I wondered if the land had given up the bulk of its natural resources long ago, overrun by too much civilization.

Saucy stood in the aisle, refusing to exchange places with me for any part of the two hour ride. We talked about plucky Annie, how she taught us by example to cross the Roman streets. All the way to Napoli I cried over losing her. How could a woman and a steamer trunk completely disappear?

HAIL COMEDIA

Phil Hahn

*Inspired by the postage stamp
honoring poet/humorist
Ogden Nash*

Let us now praise dear Ogden Nash
Great hudibrastic scamp,
Who's gone and got his puss put on
A U.S. postage stamp.

It's a long time coming,
Let's shout hooray for you
About damn time some funny folk
Have finally got their due.

Perhaps with this beginning
We can honor other wags…
Could kindly old James Thurber's face
Adorn our nation's flags?

Or, flanking Lady Liberty
In Upper New York Bay
How 'bout a new colossus
Of Perelman, S.J?

Or added to Mount Rushmore
A true comedic schtarker,
With fifty-foot pure granite head,
The late Miss Dorothy Parker.

And then, while we're about it,
The U.S. Seal, eventually
Could feature all the features of
That rascal Robert Benchley.

Ah, those would be the days, my friend,
When honors we would choose
For that risible fraternity
With talent to amuse

But no, alas, 'twon't come to pass,
Our Vision Thing needs fixin'
Just please, dear God, don't let them name
An airport after Nixon.

LOVE OFFERINGS

Faye Newman

Reverend David spoke today of bringing gifts, and as I listened, I glanced at the maple leaf pin on my sweater: gold layered upon gold, solid, yet delicately crafted. Much like the woman who left it to me.

A few weeks ago, my husband's mother died. The pin and a locket containing a miniature photograph of her son as an infant were the mementos I received upon her death. I will treasure them. They are mementos from a woman I spent 25 years hating.

Lucille was a good woman. She gave of herself all that she had to give. She was a loving wife and mother, a woman whose entire life was devoted to the care of her home and family.

Lucille's life was not easy. She suffered discord, and even abuse, during her long first marriage. Her health was often shaky. She gave birth to nine children, six of whom lived. Her nutritional disorder was misunderstood and poorly controlled and she complained so often of mysterious illnesses that her family ceased to hear.

She suffered also from severe learning disabilities, unable to read or write much more than her name. Having never known the joy to be found in a good book, she had no patience for people who read for pleasure, my typical escape from life's intolerable situations.

Arriving in San Jose as a frightened and far too young, pregnant bride, I often fled from this woman to my imaginary world, biting my nails.

We lived with his parents until we could afford a

place of our own. From the beginning, Lucille and I waged war. For the most part, it was a cold war, fought in small, silent skirmishes over little things. I'd make our bed, tucking the covers because my husband's six-foot-four-inch frame hung over the end and his feet got cold. Lucille would follow and untuck them because it looked better. I, who had never seen a clothesline, would hang the laundry. She would rearrange all the pins, removing middle clips and doubling pieces. She starched and ironed everything from pillowcases to men's briefs. I saw no sense in such excessive labor and refused to do it.

A dust mote wouldn't dare be found in her house. The whatnot drawer was organized.

Dust bunnies and I were intimately acquainted. I hated housework, having cleaned up after five brothers and a sister since I was eleven. I took every opportunity to hide and read when I could find something readable in a printed-word-free zone. She called me lazy, and worse, when she thought I couldn't hear. Her daughter, a schoolgirl my age, smirked. She did far less than was expected of me, a wife, and I could never understand the distinction.

There came a time when I spent many of my mornings being intimate with the porcelain bowl in the bathroom, wishing I could die and get it over. Lucille was anything but sympathetic.

"Now, see," she said to my sister-in-law, "if you're a good girl, that'll never happen to you." I'd have given anything to be anywhere else in the world.

On rare occasions, we forgot that our reason for being thrown together in one household was the only thing we shared: our love for her son, my husband. When we did, our war exploded into issues dividing the family. One sister-in-law told me to go back to Oregon where I belonged; the other sister told me I was nothing like what she expected for her brother; he had said I was *pretty*. Dad rode the fence.

From this rocky foundation came the shape of our future. For a quarter of a century, Lucille and I disagreed over everything and often pretended peace for the sake of the family.

I raised my children with an easy hand. She spoke dire warnings for the future of spoiled children. Yet, she loved my children as much as I did, and kept all four at every opportunity, not always a good thing. She railed at my daughter for being seen in the front yard in a bathing suit, but smiled when she caught the boys with pornography. I often felt batted back and forth like a racquetball by the peculiar polarities of her attitudes.

Yet, I did learn much from her, when I could set aside my ire. I learned there is no such thing as a permanent stain. I learned how to make grocery dollars stretch to near impossible lengths. I learned how to disassemble a garment and use it to as a pattern for new ones. I learned to hide a zipper within the folds of a skirt. I learned to recognize when a child's infection needed attention, though I was unwilling to apply her down-home remedies. I learned, for example, that a slice of salt pork taped over a boil is not a good way to 'draw the f'ar out' if you don't know that the cause of the lesion is chicken pox.

I learned about love, too, when I was willing. I watched her give her all to care for her children and theirs, leaving her own needs for last. She sewed clothes for my kids just because she wanted to do it.

Everyone had good school clothes before she bought shoes for herself, everyone chose what to watch on the tube before she did, and everyone else decided what to do on a Sunday afternoon, what to eat for dinner.

Sometimes her children rewarded her with their love, sometimes with resentment. I learned from her that both were transitory, and patience brought change. Years passed. She lost her husband, lived alone and lonely, found love and remarried in her sixties. Her son and I moved to Oregon, where I belonged. We raised her grandchildren, and saw her only occasionally, for which I was grateful.

A new marriage softened her. She began to greet me with hugs, and ask me to visit. Our one last skirmish dealt with her criticism of my new daughter-in-law, and resulted in my pouring out my alienation from the family. I told her I was determined my daughters-in-law would never feel that way.

I never saw a frown, nor heard a disparaging word about others again and realized, belatedly, that she never understood how her words affected me. From then on, she greeted me with warmth, even when she knew her son and I were apart. As she drifted away in the long, painful departure of Alzheimer's disease, I was one of two people she remembered during our visits, and would obey when I ordered her to eat.

As she lay dying, her mind disoriented, her body emaciated, her teeth too large for her shrunken face, we drove to Sacramento for her birthday celebration. Only weeks before, her family had buried her second husband, the one who was kind to her.

She knew me, though she didn't recognize all of her family, and I asked what she'd like for her birthday. I waited a very long time for her whispered answer, "Not to be hit any more."

We knew she referred not to those who cared for her now, but to the husband with whom she had passed the majority of her life, the husband I knew she had loved, who had preceded the man who treated her like a princess. The father of the son I had married.

A lump formed in my throat and I understood her as I never had, loved her as I never had.

"Oh, Mom, you know nobody ever hits you," her daughter said. But Lucille was living in the past.

"No one ever will again," I whispered, and clung to her hand for a moment. Then I escaped before I could burst into tears.

With regret, I know now that our alienation from one another resided as much in my imagination as in truth.

We were from different realities, raised with different standards. Different rules applied to women in our worlds. She did the best she could with what she had and what she knew. I know that today in a way I didn't understand while she lived.

Her son and I are separated, but I find that I did not leave his mother behind easily. Lucille was a good woman. I will treasure the many gifts she gave me, and remember all of them when I wear the Maple Leaf pin.

In this excerpt from a novel in progress Molly Carpenter looks for the chestnut trees she saw when she somehow traveled into the past.

AT A LOSS IN THE WOODS
Angela Lebakken

> *The place where you lose the trail is not necessarily the place where it ends... even the trails we find are only fragments of the trails that lie beyond our comprehension.*
> From The Tracker by William Jon Watkins

" Right here should be the chestnut. Where *are* all the chestnut trees? I guess I'm not where I thought I was," Molly said as she pivoted with her arms spread and gazed in all directions.

"Taint chestnuts in these woods anymore."

"Why? I thought I saw them everywhere."

"They used to grow all over these parts 'til 'round 1900 or sich. Then a fungus got 'em. It was drawn out, took several years but when people saw 'em dyin' off, they logged as much as they could. No matter if the tree was healthy or not. Woodpeckers, wind, rain spread the disease and man didn't give the strong trees a fightin' chance. Chestnut wood was used for 'most everything. Those split rails around that cabin, the shingles too — probably chestnut — it decays so slow. But now... well, the American Chestnut is long gone."

"But... ." She decided to keep her argument to herself, after all Beth knew what she was talking about. Had she really experienced stepping back in time? Somewhere before 1900. She knew she'd seen majestic chestnuts flourishing among oak, hickory, maple and birch. The deep, spiraling fissures in the bark of the trunk she had leaned against that day with Cat could be nothing other than a chestnut. And the ground had been thick with large nuts.

Trying to wrap her mind around this, her eyes met Beth's quizzical expression.

"Thar's a dwarf chestnut that seems immune. I don't see those here either."

"No, no. It's okay. I must have been mistaken."

Their hike led them deeper into the thick stand of trees than she had ventured before. Climbing a steep stretch they fell silent, reserving their breath for oxygen intake.

"Ah, here's ginseng nestled alongst maidenhair fern," Beth squatted and swished the fronds to one side.

"I'd have missed that. It's almost cowering now. In late fall it takes center stage. Could it be Virginia Creeper instead? ...Here I am, questioning you."

"No, you could've been right. The leaf clusters are akin. I reckon I know sang when I see it."

Molly smiled. Ginseng — sang. A little thing, but significant enough to instill a feeling of place. "So, do you harvest sang yourself?"

"Shucks, not much anymore. My mama and I useta years back."

"I gather it was considered valuable long ago."

"Oh yeah. Fer the Cherokee ginseng was the plant of life, fer all its power. And we used it fer digestion, fer energy. An all 'round tonic. Mama gave it to us girls fer cramps, too."

"The roots, right?"

Beth nodded.

As they traipsed, Molly heard the soft nasal mewing she'd mistaken for a kitten on one of her walks. "Listen," she said.

"Look," Beth pointed to a birch tree. "About mid-way. See 'em?"

She spied the birds and was twisting her pack around to pull out one of the small nature books she'd brought along when Beth continued,

"That one's a yellow-bellied sapsucker. It's a male — see his red throat? He's probing fer insects. He'll be back feeding at those same holes again."

"Guess I didn't need these books, huh?"

Beth shrugged, grinned. *There's that lipstick commercial again*, Molly thought as she took pictures. They stood silent with necks cricked and watched until the bird flew.

When they rounded a bend, a raccoon stared at them. They stared back, inching toward him. Molly and Beth beamed at each other as if they shared a delicious secret. The raccoon allowed them near enough to see his eyes peek through his mask. His size and stillness told them he was adult. They hesitated, and Molly tried to communicate with her eyes as she eased her camera up and snapped two pictures. He turned and ambled off as if saying, "I've posed long enough, get the message?"

They walked in silence for several minutes. In a hushed voice, Beth said, "You know, in lore the raccoon stands fer disguise. It's said if a raccoon happens on your path you should pay close attention. Maybe someone you know is wearing a mask, not lettin' you see who they really are. Or, you may even be hidin' from your own self."

"You mean living a lie or being lied to?"

"Well, yeah, but not like a deliberate thing. More of an unawareness."

"Or maybe like going to a masquerade ball. Hiding behind a mask. Pretending you are royalty or living out a fantasy," Molly said.

"Dressin' up and pretendin' is like knockin' on the door of another world."

"Or dimension?"

"It's worth studyin'. It's an important sign fer both of us. Most likely different fer you than me."

Another trip to the bookstore, Molly thought.

"Beth, where's the closest library? Maybe they'd have books about animal signs."

"Oh, I reckon you'd need to go to a bigger place. The libraries here are small. Though they might could order books. I know someone who... ah, here we are. The headwaters of Sugar Creek are just beyond the waterfall."

"Should we rest here and have lunch?"

"Let's climb over these boulders. Thar's a clearing at the spring. If I remember right, some nice fallen logs to sit on. Sunshine and shade to choose from."

They scrambled on and when they reached the glen, Molly plopped down on a log and untied her bootlaces. "I'm getting my feet in that stream. Now. Cool 'em off."

Beth laughed. "That's what I always do. Sometimes I strip and swim. 'Specially when it's really hot weather. Today's not too bad."

"Sounds tempting. Let's eat first. Do you ever worry about being caught naked? I had a sensation of someone watching me when I took a quick dip one day."

"Naw. Jest a few locals come up here, and they'd pay no mind."

Tiptoeing out of the creek, they sat side by side, barefoot and jeans rolled up. Like a couple of kids gone fishing. Unwrapping her tuna sandwich Molly got a whiff and half expected Cat to appear even though they were nowhere near the cabin.

"What kind of shop do you work at that can close at a moment's notice?"

"Well, I only work there two mornings a week. I jest got a divorce and I'm needin' more money," Beth said. "I'm savin' up to take some classes so I can get better work than cleanin' houses."

"Does it bother you then, losing a day's work?"

"Oh, no. My boss is so kindly. I'm sure I'll get paid fer today since he's the one who canceled."

"Nice."

Molly realized Beth hadn't told her where she worked, but didn't pursue it. They ate in comfortable silence, each to her own thoughts. During the pause, their surroundings came alive with more noise than squirrels and birds. A larger animal prowled. Beth held a finger to her mouth as they listened. Molly wondered if there were bears around here but kept still, alert, and looking for a good climbing tree. They both grinned when they heard a low human whistle. Just another explorer. Sure enough, the bushes parted and into the clearing strode a man.

"Beth," he said, "and Molly."

*The following occured on a trip researching the **The Emperor's Daughter** by Sandy Kretzschmar.*

CICERO'S POOL

Sandy Kretzschmar

The island of Ventotene, Italy

I wandered through Cicero's inn of "little problemas," looking for him. Like all his rooms, ours was new but visibly lopsided. The door wouldn't close and the windows wouldn't open. The closest bathroom down the hall had, according to Cicero, a "little problema." The toilet was plugged. The next bath further down the hall had another "little problema." The shower wasn't connected. The sink to the third "little problema" lay bottom up on the hall terracotta floor.

Following the scent of roasted red peppers, I found Cicero in his *cucina* preparing our breakfast bruschetta. *"Scuzi,"* I asked, *"ha una piscina?"* Do you have a pool? "Si, si. Pool, pool!" He motioned for me to follow, wiping his hands on his apron and waving his arms wildly, as if I were the first privileged mermaid in paradise to test the warm waters of his private lagoon.

Cicero raced through his dining room to the open patio door. Leaping into the air like a court jester, he landed outside in the morning heat. I watched him scurry up narrow whitewashed steps to the rooftop where he leaned over a short cinderblock ledge, insisting I hurry. I called out to Meggie, "At last, we're in luck. He's got a pool!"

Then I realized his steep stairs lacked a railing or an

adjoining wall where I might brace myself for the climb. I'd seen something like this before in tempting photos of villas high on the cliffs of the Amalfi Coast. Bleached by searing sun and unrestrained sea breezes, they nudged a sense of longing within me. Julia had climbed whitewashed steps to rooftops a thousand times, and I hadn't realized it until this moment.

"Piscina, piscina!" Cicero sang. Pool, pool! He twirled in delight, flinging his arms wide and tossing his head back into bright Mediterranean sunlight, elated to show off his pool.

I'd carried my new slenderizing bathing suit around Italy and two rocky-shore islands for three weeks without getting it wet. Meggie and I had explored the ancient ruins of thermal baths in Rome, Pompeii and Herculaneum. The only modern pools I'd seen were locked behind the high gates of hotels I couldn't afford. Cicero's stairs looked hazardous. But I'd risk them for a pool.

I took one cautious step and then another until I stood beside Cicero on the roof. A vast expanse of black tar paper covered the flat rooftop with no pool in sight. He explained in Italian babble and made-up sign language that since the outside walls of Villa Serena extended three feet higher than the roof he would flood the entire rooftop thus making a shallow pool the same size as the building beneath.

Cicero assured me that in three months he would have a pool. It will, of course, leak through his cinder block roof into the kitchen, dining room, and apartments below if the sheer weight doesn't collapse his construction completely, washing all his "little problemas" over dry grass and prickly pear meadows down to the sea.

Meggie met me at the patio door, bathing suit in hand.

"Never mind," I said. "He's a little bit crazy."

She shook her head in disgust and we returned to our room, walking the long hall that veered to the right like a listing, sinking boat. "His parents must have had high hopes for him," she said, "naming him after the great Cicero."

"No, they were right. I don't know much Latin. But Cicero means — chickpea."

Back in our lopsided room, Meggie tossed her swimsuit into her bag with a sigh. "I'm starving," she said. "Let's hope his cooking isn't another "little problema."

NO PROBLEMA BRUSCHETTA
An Italian country dish from the island of Ventotene

4 to 6 sweet red peppers
6 tablespoons olive oil
1 large onion, diced
1 large melanzana (eggplant), peeled and diced
1 tablespoon crushed garlic
1/3 cup chopped fresh basil leaves
1 tablespoon chopped fresh oregano
1 tablespoon balsamic vinegar
1 teaspoon fresh lemon juice
Bakery-fresh bread, Italian or French

Dressing
1/4 cup olive oil
1/2 cup lemon juice,
2 tablespoons balsamic vinegar

1. Trim tops from red peppers and slice in quarters. Broil peppers, skin side up, until skins turn black. Remove from oven, cover with aluminum foil to cool. The steam will loosen the pepper skins for easy peeling. Peel the peppers and cut or tear into strips.
2. Sautè in olive oil: onion, eggplant, garlic, basil, oregano, 1 tablespoon vinegar, 1 teaspoon fresh lemon juice.
3. Spoon mixture atop toasted, sliced, bakery-fresh Italian or French bread. Add red pepper.
4. Make dressing and drizzle over mixture and bread. Makes four to six servings. Recipe may be cut in half.

Buon Appetito!

APPLES AND CINNAMON

Faye Newman

Apples and cinnamon. That's what I smell in the fall. It's the fragrance hanging in the air from the dessert I made for dinner, so redolent of a hot August day in Montana as my brother and mother and I drove back from Wyoming. The sun was setting on the Big Sky as we entered the crowded restaurant and were seated. Dessert that day was fried apples, too, with the rich taste of real butter and a little sugar and a lot of cinnamon.

I am sad as I drink in the lovely fragrance. We'd spent a week with Mom's youngest brother, Irvin, and his wife, Aunt Wilma, with whom I have since kept up a correspondence. I fell in love with the two of them that week: Irvin, nearing eighty, with his wry sense of humor stirring insides and tickling rather than giving you a belly laugh like Aunt Wilma does.

Earthy and maybe even a little raunchy beneath a prim, stylish exterior, Aunt Wilma is around ten years younger than Uncle Irvin and they've been holding hands and looking dreamily at each other for half a century. A good marriage, strong, full of the richness of time, that's what the scent of apples and cinnamon evoke for me.

I think I'll go outside now, and soak up the scent of the volunteer pine tree in my border and the salty, fishy tang of the ocean I can see from here, and let the wind dry the tears the scent of apples and cinnamon bring to my eyes.

Uncle Irvin died this week. Thank you, God, for the gift of knowing my Uncle Irvin and Aunt Wilma and the fragrance of apples and cinnamon.

HOME IS
Angela Lebakken

Yesterday I strode the beach
and the sweet smoke of a bonfire unseen
filled my nostrils, moved my mind
to a land far away
I once declared home.
Marshmallows turn golden then black
Mingling vanilla and charcoal.
Hot dogs on sticks — crackling spices.
Leaves burning, marshmallows, too.
North Dakota — my childhood home.

Yesterday I roasted chilies
and a yearning welled up
pounding my heart
propelling my mind
to a land far away
I once declared home.
This piquant aroma
permeating the air — everywhere.
Roasting red chilies and green.
New Mexico — home for a season.

Today I trek into the woods.
Damp, decomposing fills my senses.
My mind wonders not.
I declare this my home.
Rich, rotting leaves, gentle rain.
Mushrooms like teacups in shades of brown
turned right side up and upside down.
I inhale odors of fusty fungi.
Oregon — home for good reason.

Tomorrow's dream and Autumn essence
 — pungent, sweet, spicy — blending,
wafting to me.
Guiding my mind
to a land yet unknown.
Will it, one day, be home?
Aroma memories touch my heart
Dusty leaves, smoky fires, earthy air
My home is — anywhere.

A CHANGE IN THE AIR

Phil Hahn

You *can tell it's fall with your eyes shut*, Earl thought as he tripped the lever on the old Farmall, and the plow dropped down, digging into the dusty stubble, turning it over to rich, black loam. Fresh-plowed ground has an unmistakable smell, "a yeasty, crisp, full-bodied nose," a wine connoisseur might say. Aged, bottled beneath the sod 'til it becomes a vintage brew... uncorked by the shares of the plow to gently kiss the nostrils with the scent of life-to-come.

Earl settled the right front wheel into the furrow so the venerable tractor actually steered itself, and closed his eyes. *Yep, that's fall all right* he smiled to himself. Dried leaves of oak and cottonwood gave off a spicy gingersnap perfume... an old Macintosh tree sent its applesauce scent to caress his eager nostrils... from the riverbank half a mile away, a faint wisp of dying milkweed, thistle, and sunflower. They made him sneeze in the summer, but

now they made him grin. From somewhere south he could smell the first fall fire from an iron stove... *wood smoke in autumn,* Tennessee Williams had recalled in *The Glass Menagerie.* The words so graceful, they imparted a fragrance that was almost palpable.

It was good to come home from the city to help out with the plowing. Dad always appreciated it, and that warmed his heart. But the truth was, Earl had always loved to plow. It was fall, the end of old life and the start of new. This field, once plowed, would be harrowed and weeded, disced and cultivated, kept clean of growth so the soil could rest, could sleep like some great snoring bear, sleep to regenerate, sleep to dream, 'til the crocuses whisper it awake to serve once more.

It was good to plow. It was good to help out. It was good to come home to the soil and the fall.

*This is another excerpt from Ina Christensen's memoir **A White Stone**.*

CHURCH, LIGHT, AND MAPLE BARS

Ina Christensen

Like the school, the church at Vaughn is very small. It sits next to the grocery store, on the bank above the millpond. Skunk cabbage grows in marshy land behind the building. The smell, together with rotting debris from the millpond, gives the service an odor I have come to identify as unique to the church. The church is too small and too poor to have a minister, so the deacons hire students from Northwest Christian College in Eugene to deliver sermons on Sunday. After morning services, one family takes the speaker to their home and feeds him. Another service is offered on Sunday evening.

I always attend both services. Having different speakers each week makes me feel like I'm attending different churches. There's not a lot of hell and brimstone sermons, so I usually go home with a good feeling. Sunday night is my favorite service. With the muted light and the candles, the shabby room looks cozy and warm.

Sunday nights, Dad is home with Mama because he has to work the next day. I like to share the day's message with Mama. I'm always hoping she will jump in and give her opinion on the sermon like she used to with Aunt Sera, but she never does. She's sitting on the couch with Dad when I come in. Dad will have an arm around her neck, with his hand inside the front of her dress. This is old stuff, so I pay no attention. When Dad is home he is either feeling Mama's boobs, or stroking her butt. *Mama says Dad puts a lot of store in good sex. I think that means he likes it. I think Mama must think that it's pretty important too because that's what she usually wants to talk about.*

Mama doesn't say anything when I tell her my version of the sermon, but Dad snorts and rolls his eyes, and that makes me mad. Where does he get the nerve to make fun of a Christian when he isn't even baptized? I know that because I hear Mama talking to him about it all the time. Mama tells Dad, if he gets killed before he is baptized, he'll end up in hell. I can't imagine anyone taking the chance on going to hell just because they don't like church.

I wait for Mama to say something, not just sit there with Dad's hand on her butt. I know Mama worries about going to hell and stuff, and I'm wondering if God will get mad at Mama for sitting there not saying anything while Dad makes fun of the church. I feel myself getting scared and mad inside, and before I can put a stop to my mouth, I start delivering my own sermon. I usually don't talk much to anyone other than my inside self, but every once in a while, something will get me so stirred up my mouth takes off without waiting for my brain. Mama calls it diarrhea of the mouth.

I see Mama's eyes grow big, and she shakes her head no. She wants me to stop right now before I make her lose face in front of Dad. It's almost as though I'm on the outside of myself looking on and I can't seem to put a halt on my mouth. I hate it when I'm made to look stupid so I keep on talking. I tell Dad that Noah's ark has been found, and the men who found the ark even found a pile of burned wood where Noah built an altar, and offered a burnt offering to God. I soon run out of everything I've heard the minister say, so I start making up stuff as I go along. Mama finally wiggles loose from Dad's hold and grabs my arm. She pulls me into the bedroom.

"Why do you keep acting this way? You know it only makes your dad mad."

"Why does he roll his eyes and make fun of me, then?"

"If you don't like it here, young lady, maybe it's time for you to build your own nest." Mama sits on the end of my bed, arms crossed over her chest. "Kyle Rodgers stopped by the other day when I was working in the garden. He told me he asked you to marry him. Why didn't you tell me?"

"I don't want to marry Kyle Rodgers, Mama."

"Well, from the sound of things tonight, maybe you should think about it."

"Mama, I'm only thirteen. I won't graduate from the eighth grade until June."

"Then you better learn to keep your mouth shut around your dad. I declare, Ina, isn't my life hard enough without you adding your two cents worth?"

"I'm sorry, Mama."

"Well, you should be. I'd better get back to your dad." Mama pauses at the door and turns around. "I don't know why you couldn't have been born more like Ida."

"I try Mama, honest. You shouldn't have given me Grandma's name. Maybe then Grandma wouldn't have died. I don't like having a name that belongs to someone else. Who knows, if I had my own name, I might be different."

"That's enough, Ina; I don't want to hear another word from you. You were born, your grandmother died, that's the end of it. Go to bed. Tomorrow is a school day."

I see the tears pool in Mama's eyes as she leaves the

room. I feel wicked, and I know Mama is shamed by my behavior. I promise God and myself I'll try harder to be more like Ida.

I really do try to watch my mouth. Mama thinks I don't care what people think and say about me, but that's not true. It's only that sometimes I think about things and come up with answers that are different than I'm suppose to have. When that happens, I end up making someone mad, usually Dad or the church.

One Sunday our speaker gives his sermon on man's inability to serve God and God's retribution. He reads stories from the Bible about God telling someone to kill everyone in the tribe, including all the women and children. The story really disturbs me, and I'm thinking, that's not fair. Why should everyone have to die, even if they are innocent? Then I say to myself, if I can figure this out, and I'm still a kid, then God who knows everything can figure it out, too. Next Sunday, I share my theory with my Sunday School teacher.

She is horrified that I would even dare question the word of God.

She says the Bible is from God, and therefore it is impossible to have mistakes. I think about the love that I felt when Jesus came, and the trust I feel for the guardian voice that lives in my heart. All the questions jumble together in my mind, and I don't know what the answer is. But I think maybe my teacher is wrong. She asks the class to pray for me. *I've learned from that mistake that no one is allowed to say anything bad about the church ever. Never again do I want the whole Sunday school class on their knees praying for my redemption just because I said God wouldn't ask us to kill little babies. I still don't think He would but I'm sure not going to say so.*

I still attend both services each Sunday but I'm careful about what I say when I'm in church or at home.

For example, the story the young minister shared about baptism. He was talking about how important it is to be baptized, because you never know when you're going to die. I always get a little scared when a minister talks about dying, and what will happen, if you're not one of God's own. I worry about Dad, because I know how unhappy it will make Mama, to look down from heaven, and see Dad suffering. The minister says a group of them from his dorm performed a baptism in a bathtub. He said everything went fine until the floor counselor returned. The group of them had to get the man dressed, and out of the house before they were caught. The man they had baptized was a black man, and only white men were allowed in the dorm. *If I were the black man I would wonder why God's people don't know better. I'm not about to say so, though.* At home, I usually go straight to bed. That way I figure I'll stay out of trouble.

Not everyone in camp attends the local church. Some go to Noti or Veneta; a few drive into Eugene for services. There are others who refuse to go to church at all. In Oklahoma, most people say they are religious whether they are or not, because it's expected of them. In camp, no one seems to think it strange if someone gets drunk on a Saturday night and sleeps in on Sunday morning.

I like the potluck dinner that's held once a month. Not only is the food good, it's also different from what Mama cooks which is mostly pinto beans and fried potatoes. I don't think Mama likes to cook because she usually cooks the same sort of stuff for every meal. I asked her once why she doesn't get herself a cookbook and try to cook something different. She shrugged her shoulders and said Dad likes things the way they are.

Mrs. Hickcock lives down the road from us and goes to church every Sunday. She tries to be a good Christian to everyone. She acts the way I think a good Christian should. I go to her house almost every Sunday because she fixes a big dinner with lots of great food. It's almost as good as the monthly potluck. One Sunday afternoon at a church potluck, I pile my plate high with fruit salad. Mrs. Hickock says it's Waldorf salad. It has apples and nuts, and a lot of other things. I'm ready to go back for a second helping when my arms start to itch. I'm scratching like crazy when big round hives the size of quarters pop up all over my body. I'm afraid I have a terrible disease. I jump up from the table and run all the way home. Mama takes a look, and says I have an allergy to the salad. I ask her if that is anything like my ear infection, but she says no, this is different. I won't be able to eat Waldorf salad.

Sometimes, I wonder what it would be like to go to another church, but most of the time the Vaughn church is okay. All the preachers are young and I like that. If a guy is really cute, sometimes the girls get to giggling and making so much noise Mrs. Hickock, or one of the other ladies, tells us to stop our noise or leave. We usually settle down, but most of us are paying more attention to the cute minister than to the sermon, hoping he will notice us. All the other girls are prettier than I am so they don't think I have a chance of getting him to notice me. I don't either, but that doesn't stop me from dreaming.

I still borrow books from Mr. and Mrs. Makiner, but since I started reading movie magazines the books are no longer as much fun as reading about Lana Turner or Ava Gardner. I think the Makiners' are disappointed I've switched to magazines when I could be reading Zane Grey. They don't understand how important it is to fit in, to be like everyone else. I learn lots of stuff by reading the magazines. Like, Lana has big boobs too, and seems proud of them.

I start wearing sweaters and stand in front of the mirror to practice looking sexy. There's not much I can do about my face, it's covered with freckles. I think I will just have to live with the ugly things and then I see an ad in the magazine about the wonders of pancake makeup, I know I have to try it. I save my babysitting money until I have enough to buy a compact of Max Factor pancake makeup. According to the ads it will cover anything and make you look beautiful. That's why the next time Peg Morningdove invites me along when her family goes to Eugene, I say yes.

Peg's mama gives me a funny look as I climb into the back seat along with Peg. *I wonder if Peg has asked her mama's permission to bring me along. I sit very quiet and don't say anything because I really want to go to Eugene.*

I know the routine; the car is parked in the public parking lot and everyone scatters agreeing to meet back at the lot at four. Peg and I go through Woolworth and Newberrys. I find the counter with Max Factor makeup. Peg helps me choose a color and we both agree it will be dark enough to hide my freckles. It takes all my money but it's worth it to be beautiful. Peg stops at the lunch counter and asks me if I'm having lunch. I tell her I'm not hungry and will meet her outside.

On our way home, Peg's Mama stops at a store and Peg's sister runs inside while the rest of us stay in the car. I sit quietly stroking my precious sack of beauty lying in my lap. Ellen comes back holding a flat box. As soon as she is in the car, she starts handing out small, brick shaped pastry covered with a pale brown topping. She hands me one, along with a paper napkin. It smells so good it starts my mouth to watering. I was too excited to eat breakfast this morning, and the odor sets my stomach to growling. I hold the soft, fragrant pastry to my nose, enjoying the smell. Peg jabs me in the ribs with her elbow.

"Aren't you going to eat it?" she says with her

mouth full.

"What is it?"

"It's a maple bar, silly. Haven't you ever eaten a maple bar?"

"I probably have, but I forgot." I feel bad about lying, but I don't want to be laughed at. I'm almost afraid to bite into it because how can anything smelling so wonderful taste as good as it smells. I was once given a pretzel and was thrilled by its shape, then, when I took a bite and found out it was nothing but a pretty twisted cracker, I was disappointed. This time though, I'm not, it does taste as good as it smells. What a grand day, I have something to cover my freckles and a special treat.

The next morning, I put on my tightest sweater. I set my hair up in pin curls last night, so even though my hair is a yucky brown instead of blond or brunette, at least it's curly. Using the little sponge from the pancake makeup I spread it on thick enough to cover all my flaws, including my freckles. All the way to the church, I practice walking like a movie star. Judging from the stares I'm getting, I think I must be doing it right.

We have another new speaker; a young man I've never seen before. I try to listen to what he is saying, but I can feel eyes on me. *No one is looking at me like they think I'm beautiful. Oh God, don't let me make the same mistake I made when I oiled my hair. It took me months to live that down. My inside self thinks I have made the same mistake.*

I always listen when Mama gives out beauty advice because I know she worries about me getting a husband. Mama is very proud of her hair. She wears it in one long braid at home and wound around her head when she goes anywhere. When she tells me she always oiled her hair as a girl, I think I should oil mine, too. The only oil I can find in the house is cod liver oil, so I use that. After I oil my hair thoroughly, I go to school. As soon as I see a couple of kids grab their noses, I know I've made a mistake. I tell the teacher I'm not feeling well and go home.

Now, it looks like I've screwed up again. Mrs. Hickcock doesn't say anything about my makeup, but she refuses to look at me and her lips are pressed tight so I know she is angry. All I wanted to do is be pretty.

I wash most of the makeup off before I return to evening service. I'm glad I'm the only one from my group attending. I take church seriously and refuse to stay home even though I'm still embarrassed about the makeup. I guess life in a logging camp is different than it is in Hollywood.

The young preacher is cute. I'm paying more attention to the way he looks than what he is saying. I'm more or less daydreaming when I notice a faint glow coming from behind the podium. This gets my attention, and I sit up straight. I take a quick look around the room, but no one is acting as though something unusual is happening. I have given up on seeing Jesus again, so when I see the light, I feel my heart beat faster. After all this time He is coming back. The light doesn't rise, but comes into focus. I wait for the preacher to vanish and Jesus to appear, but it doesn't happen. The light continues to become sharper and sharper until it merges together above his head. I can see him clearly. The light glows and dances above his head, but there is no music or feeling of intense love. It's alive, but not breathing. Jesus isn't coming after all. I feel such a profound loss and disappointment, I burst into sobs. I'm always so careful not to cry in public, but I have no control. I'm on the verge of hysterics, and still I cry. The young preacher leaves the podium and comes to sit beside me, adding to my humiliation.

"Is there anything I can do?" he asks.

I shake my head. I don't want to talk to anyone. I just want to go home. First, I make myself a laughing stock by thinking I could be pretty, and now, because I see things others can't, I've made everything worse. It will be all over camp by tomorrow. Crazy Ina getting weirder by the day. I don't think even a new name could help me now.

THE DANCE GOES ON

Angela Lebakken

A younger me
infatuated
with what might be.
Pulse pounding,
grinding hips
danced the dance of intensity.

A bow, a curtsy.
The minuet.
The slow dance
a quiet romance.
Gazing into his soft blues
we glide.

High kicking,
breath taking.
Whirling, spinning, laughing.
Out of control — almost.
I square dance
innocently.
And the dance goes on.

He is there and
with a shy smile
into his arms I promenade.
Dancing the hoedown
while longing
for a day sublime
and romance in three-quarter time.

THE ZOO
Ina Christensen

Narrow pinched spaces
Dancing bars of broken light
The tiger paces.

AFRICAN CATS
Phil Hahn

We should never play poker with African cats,
They are almost certain to beat us.
For a great many of them are lion…
And most of the rest are cheetahs.

ANWAR SADAT
Sandy Kretzschmar

It was my privilege to stand beside you.
Your history created a new Egypt.
Some said you were the return of
Akhenaten.
And I believed them.

A stranger took our picture to prove
My good fortune,
How I found you standing tall,
In your peacetime suit,
In the wax museum.

GRANDMOTHER'S VOICE

Faye Newman

My grandmother's voice shimmered and danced
A tremulous hummingbird
Tasting the colors of memory.
Sometimes a rainbow, soothingly tidy,
As often kaleidoscopic
Scrambled chips
Creating illusional patterns.

Crimson rose's blood-red hues
Evoke our births,
While stark white daisies
Summon oft-imagined purity of
A multitude of brides.
Her voice paused.

A smile announced another color's thought.
Perhaps the golden honeymoon cruise.
Fiery orange of angry words,
Lavender love lost and kissed good-bye
Sweet face of an infant,
Laid to rest.

My grandmother's voice had much to say.

This story is an excerpt from my still-to-be-completed family memoir. My mother, Nell Cross-Graves, born in 1900, wrote of her childhood experiences as a member of a large family living on a cattle ranch near California's Mojave Desert. I have edited her writing while remaining true to her voice. My story, following hers, takes place in the same locale years later.

GATES ACROSS TIME
Betty Wetzel

Nell - 1909

"Come on Nell! Claude and Clifford are waiting for us!" my ten-year old sister Merle shouted impatiently.

Our brothers, age thirteen and full of their own importance, cut me no slack even though I was the youngest. Merle and I knew the twins were not happy about having to work with their two younger sisters. How could we be of help in such a responsible task as the annual fall wood gathering? Our dad had said we were to work together on gathering the wood. There was no arguing with his decision. But the twins didn't have to like it.

We knew our work kept the family warm and the cookstove hot for all those delicious meals our mother prepared. The firewood came from the woods on our ranch where tall pines towered above every other tree. The Indians, working for our father, cut some of these pines into four-foot lengths and stacked this firewood in cords among the remaining pines for a season. Our job was to get these dry cords hauled to the woodshed before the rainy season. Pine-scented wood, impregnated with resin and pitch, to this day brings back pleasant memories. On Saturdays during fall, the boys hitched the two horses to the tall, sturdy old wooden wagon and we four drove through the fields to load wood and then stack it in our woodshed. It took many wagonloads to fill.

This particular fall, Merle and I argued with the boys every trip about who would open and close the large wire gates as we drove the team through field after field. It took both of us girls to open and close each gate. We wanted to pair one twin with one sister. Each twin could handle the gates without help. The twins haughtily assigned Merle and me gate duty going for the wood and decreed they, together, opened gates on the return trip. That meant the boys drove the team and empty wagon at a brisk pace while going for the wood and Merle and I drove the team and wood-filled wagon slowly, ploddingly, home.

"It's not fair," Merle and I protested, "you boys are bigger and stronger and should help us open the gates."

They laughed, punching each other in the ribs, and mimicking our protests back to us. Merle and I sat, legs dangling over the rear bed of the wagon, sulking. In sullen silence, we jumped to the ground at the first gate, walking toward the front of the wagon, beyond the two horses, to wrestle the gate open. The half-dozen or so fields we drove through each held from forty to a hundred head of cattle, mostly Herefords, brought in from open range where they had grazed all summer. Our ranch was located just on the outskirts of the Mojave Desert, in a small valley sustained by water from the Kern River. Dad and his cowhands had recently rounded up the cattle from the high Sierra meadows where they fed all summer. The cattle were split into smaller groups and left in the outlying fenced fields surrounding the ranch complex. There they would settle down a little before they were brought on in to the home pasture for the winter, when feeding would be necessary.

Sometimes, after Merle and I jumped from the wagon and opened a gate, our brothers would drive the wagon through and keep on going for a ways while we wrestled the gate closed. As we trudged toward the wagon, those untamed range cattle frightened us with their curiosity. They sauntered in our direction. They pursued us. If we walked fast, they gained by walking faster and if we ran, they ran along with us. We didn't dare stand still or they would circle us. Finally, we reached the safety of the wagon. Claude and Clifford always had a good laugh at our fears.

"Come on, you sissies. You know those cattle will run from any sudden noise. Just scream at them like you do at us," Claude hooted. And he and Clifford roared with laughter as they urged the team forward.

Our dad had warned all of us not to shoot a gun or yell near the range cattle, despite the boys' teasing us to shout at them, because the cattle might stampede.

Merle and I plotted a long time to get even with our brothers. Finally, we got them to agree to let us open the gates on the return trip, when the wagon was heavy with wood and slow moving. That meant Merle and I drove the team and empty wagon on the trip out. As we headed through the brown, dusty fields that morning, the horses were fresh and trotted fast. Merle and I waited until we were nearly to the woods, which lay just beyond the last and biggest field. At the far end of this field the dry grass and sagebrush gave way to thinly spaced groupings of small trees.

The herd of fifty or so grazing cattle looked up and kept their eyes on us as we clucked at the horses to pull the wagon through the gate and into the field. When we hadn't made any move to leave Claude and Clifford behind at the first several gates, they became a little careless, taking their time closing the gate into this last big field.

Merle flashed a brief grin, "Let's do it!" She faced forward and shouted "Gee-Up" to the horses as she urged them on with the reins. I slapped that old whip toward their backs with all my strength. "Heyaa!" I chortled happily, not to be left out.

We quickly left Claude and Clifford in the dust - yelling and cussing us - as we trotted on to the last gate, on the outskirts of the woods. We waited there for the boys. They didn't come. We couldn't see very far back because of the trees and the slight slope we had come down. Merle reined the horses and wagon around and drove back about a half-mile and still we couldn't see them. Now concerned, we urged the horses on, back toward the gate where we had left the twins.

When we neared the gate we saw a big bull down on his knees butting the ground as if in a mad fury. Dust flying everywhere; his bellows of rage sending shivers down our backs to the tips of our toes. Cattle surrounded the bull in a semicircle. No boys to be seen. Had the bull killed them? We had the rifle, so Merle handed me the reins and shot up in the air. The cattle stirred restlessly.

As we approached closer, Merle fired over the heads of the cattle again and then fired into the ground near them.

Cattle bawled, broke and ran right at us, frightening our horses. As one, both horses lunged forward into a run, veering away from the approaching cattle, bouncing Merle and me and the empty wagon through the field. The bawling cattle directly behind us, we raced toward a small grove of trees. Merle somehow managed to fire in the air again; the cattle swerved right and thundered past the wagon.

Through all this, I was frozen in place, reins tightly clinched in both fists, pulling with all my nine-year old strength. Now, with Merle also pulling on the reins, we somehow managed to slow and then stop the horses. The trees were directly in front of us. Shaken and somber, we turned the team around and trotted back to the gate. Our brothers were standing there! They had never looked better to us. All animosities and challenges were momentarily forgotten.

The boys said the cattle, with the bull leading, started running toward them. They both scrambled under the fence and rolled down into a big irrigation ditch with a head gate where they hid. In the scramble, Claude lost his hat, which the bull gored and tore to pieces.

Then and there we made a pact never to leave each other at a gate again because someone could have been killed by our foolish pranks. We also agreed we didn't want our father ever to learn what we had done and we prayed fervently that no one had heard the shots.

* * *

I finish typing Mother's story into the computer and am left with questions. Did the incident really happen? If so, did it occur as she remembers it? It rings true to me in many details as I call to mind the horseback ride my cousin, Little Clifford, and I took one day. It began at the ranch managed by his father, Big Clifford, one of the twin brothers from my mother's gate story. It ended at our grandparents' home, several miles away. And it occurred in the same Kern River valley where my mother's story took place.

Betty - 1941

Little Clifford and I were eight or nine. Our legs were too short to reach the stirrups from the ground, strain as we might. We had to use a stool or fence to mount our horses. Did we saddle our own horses? Later, yes, but at this age, I can't recall. I do remember wrestling a saddle onto the back of an old, gentle mare many times by positioning the horse next to a fence where the saddle hung over a rail. Once the saddle was on, the next challenge was to cinch it tight enough that it wouldn't slip under her belly when I mounted. That old mare knew enough to inhale when I cinched and exhale only after I had exerted every bit of my strength to tighten the cinch. Somehow she even managed not to exhale until I was safely astride. Several times, I led my horse home, saddle askew, because she had outwitted me again.

I was staying for several days with my aunt and uncle, as I did every summer. Their ranch had no electricity or telephone, but no one thought this any lack, or at least we children didn't. I thought it was fun going to bed by lantern light and awakening early the next morning for a new day's adventure. Little Clifford and I had been getting into a bit of mischief, I suppose.

The day was hot and dry. My cousin and I slipped quietly from the fenced yard surrounding the house, running toward the windmill in the center of the corral, which was full of milling, bawling, range cattle. We had been told to stay in the yard when cattle were in this large corral. As I think back on this parental warning, nothing had changed from the wild cattle admonitions given by my grandparents to their children so many years earlier.

Crawling through the rail fence surrounding the vibrating windmill, we stomped in the cool overflow from the tank far above, splashing in the water and making a muddy mess of ourselves. When we tired of that, we decided to run back across the corral into the yard. The curious cattle had moved in to observe us. Now they stood shoulder-to-shoulder between us and the safety of the yard. We suddenly realized we were cut off, marooned, in the middle of the corral. We couldn't call Aunt Trudy to rescue us; she'd give us a scolding. Uncle Clifford was working in the fields somewhere; we knew we wouldn't dare call him, either.

Little Clifford and I dared each other to run across the corral, away from the house and the cattle, toward the barn and smaller pens. We scampered across the hot, dusty corral, arrived breathless beside the barn. Looking back, our escape aroused no interest from the cattle; they were still bunched between the house and the windmill, staring intently toward the windmill. Peering into one of the smaller holding pens, a wooden corral perhaps fifteen feet square, we saw a lone Hereford, a whiteface calf. Although the calf was obviously being kept in isolation for a reason, we didn't think about that.

Cliff shouted, "Let's ride him."

"No! Not me! I won't. He's three or four hundred pounds of mean, not a 90-pound baby. He'll clobber me! I don't want to be a rodeo star. I'll get bucked off or fall off and you'll laugh at me."

"Well, fraidy-cat. I'm going to ride that calf. Here,

help me hold him, at least."

Cliff abruptly grabbed the calf by the tail and gave a sharp twist. Bawling loudly in protest the calf headed full speed for a corner, Cliff clinging gamely to the tail as he was dragged behind.

"Here, Betty! Hold his head down," Cliff commanded.

The calf outweighed me. Shutting my eyes, I grimly held on to his neck, arms wrapped tight, fingers grasping reddish-brown hair, holding my breath against the sweet-sour pungency emanating from the calf. Cliff swung astride. The calf let out a mighty bellow, knocking me aside, and kicked and bucked across the pen. Cliff clung on. The calf, still bellowing, ran straight at the fence, swerving at the last instant, ramming Cliff's leg along the fence. He bucked back to the center of the pen where, abruptly, Cliff shot from his back, hitting the ground backside first. His rump landed in a pile of very runny cow-dung. I stood nearby, helpless to stop my peals of laughter.

"Oh, boy. Look at you. Some cowboy you are. What a mess!"

Cliff slowly got to his feet, wiping the goo from his jeans, with a look of disgust. Then he glared at me, laughing at him.

"Laugh at me, will you..."

He reached down, grabbed a large handful of cow-dung and flung it at my head. That stopped the laughter. It hit me in the ear and the side of the head. And it hurt! I began to cry. Cliff sobered. We helped each other begin to clean up. We needed water, lots of water. My ear and my braids were full of sticky dung. And his jeans — let's say he'd never be allowed in the house with them on.

We ran back across the corral, ignoring the cattle and crawled through the rail fence around the windmill once more. My hands shook; I couldn't begin to get my braids clean. I finally had to let my hair loose, knowing I'd never be able to braid it again well enough to pass Aunt Trudy's scrutiny. It was then we noticed Aunt Trudy, hand on hip, watching us from the front steps of the house. Wielding her broom like a sword, she marched into the corral, 'shushing' cattle to the right and the left as she approached us. With a handhold on each child, she marched us back through those cattle. They parted like the Red Sea before us. We were led safely ashore, through those Herefords, into the yard surrounding the house. When Aunt Trudy finished with us, my ears were sore from more than the dung that had been not so gently removed. We each got an earful of admonitions on the dangers of running through the corral and riding that sick calf. Later, Uncle Clifford heard about our escapades and we received another lecture. We were two meek kids as we slunk off to bed.

The next morning my mother stopped by on her way to visit her parents. That was when Little Clifford and I had our wonderful idea. We would ride horses to our grandparents' for a visit. My mother would let them know we were on our way. I'm still not sure why everyone agreed so readily, but soon Cliff and I were astride saddled horses, complete with a packed lunch and good wishes from our families. Not to mention lots of instructions to go straight to our grandparents' home, not to dawdle, and above all, to close every gate as we rode through the fields because they held cattle.

We dawdled, exploring every side trail and every unusual sound. Rabbits scurried into their burrows, field mice chittered and scrambled beneath sage, a horned frog blinked lazily at us from his perch on a fence post. We checked the number of blackbirds squabbling in a dead cottonwood tree. We whistled at the resting cattle, just to see them get to their feet and turn toward us as we passed. At the first gate, Cliff led his horse up close, leaned far out and raised the top wire noose holding the gatepost to the fence post, letting the gate flop back on itself. He guided his horse carefully over the downed gate. I followed close behind. Once in the next pasture, we realized we had a problem. There was no way to reach that downed gate and set it in place again without dismounting. Cliff jumped down, wrestled the gate into position, and slipped the wire back over the end post.

"Not so tough," he reported smugly.

Cliff led his horse to a low stump nearby, which he used as a step. He clambered up into his saddle. The second gate was a little harder to open and close. Cliff had to dismount just to open it. Since there was no stump nearby, he positioned his horse beside the fence, climbed up the barbed cross-wires and remounted.

The third gate took more muscle than Cliff had. I dismounted to help him. He squeezed with both arms around the gatepost and fence post to give enough slack so I could slip the wire up over the top of the gatepost. It took half-a-dozen tries before we forced the wire back over both gateposts. We remounted by climbing the wire fence and bringing our horses close enough to grab for the saddles and swing astride.

Each succeeding gate seemed to present a new and different challenge. I remember one particularly stubborn gate. We worked and worked and still couldn't get it open. We considered turning around, but the thought of all those gates we had already opened and closed stopped us. Finally we opened the gate, but soon realized there was no way, even working in unison, we had enough muscle to force the wire back over the gatepost. Cliff took out his pocketknife, cut a length of rope from his pack and secured the gatepost with a rope noose. We knew we would have to tell Uncle Clifford about that before it broke.

We weren't dawdling any more. All we could think of was getting to the end of the ride. We stopped near a downed tree to rest and eat lunch. Reluctantly, we mounted our horses once again, using the downed tree as our step. The horses, however, were becoming a bit impatient with this entire stopping, dismounting and remounting. By the next gate, I firmly believed they had conspired with each other. Neither would stand quietly next to a fence to be mounted. As Cliff or I reached out for the saddle, our horse sidestepped just out of reach. We finally gave up trying to remount and walked the horses to the next gate.

It must have been late afternoon when we came within sight of the river and our grandparents' home beyond. As we approached, we saw our grandmother waiting for us. Cliff and I each called to her, our voices intertwined.

"Grandma, I'm tired."

"I need a drink of water."

"My butt is sore."

"Do you have any cookies?"

"These stupid horses wouldn't stand still."

She shouted, "Where have you two been? You know you were to come straight here! Why didn't you answer me when I called and called you?"

Clifford and I tried to explain about the gates and that we had never once heard her calling us. She was too upset to hear our excuses and accused us of ignoring her calls. She had become so worried she insisted Granddad drive his car to Uncle Clifford's to see if, for some reason, we had decided not to ride over. Granddad's arrival at the ranch caused concern. We had left several hours earlier. Now neither family knew where we were, except somewhere between the ranch and the grandparents' house in one of those cattle-filled fields. Were we hurt? Or lost? Uncle Clifford drove his truck back over, following his father, expecting the worst, only to find we had arrived safely, albeit late. Very late. Barely greeting us, except to acknowledge our presence, he turned around and drove back to the ranch to let Aunt Trudy and the rest of the cousins know we had completed our journey safely.

I have no memory of how or exactly when Little Clifford and I returned to the ranch. I do know we didn't ride through all those fields with all those fences and gates again, ever.

COALY
Phil Hahn

I knew a horse, called "Coaly," 'cause
His coat was total black.
We rode him with no saddle then,
Sat right down on his back.

Old Coaly, gentle patient horse,
Tall and strong and wide;
No plows to pull, 'cause tractors came,
So he gave kids a ride.

We'd ride him, kick him
In the flanks to try to make him run,
But Coaly knew us kids'd fall
So he just had his fun.

Giving gentle rides to boys
Pretending they were bigger
Like Hoppy, glued to Blackjack's back,
Or even Roy, on Trigger.

He'd pulled a plow some years before,
His furrow straight, and square,
Folks paid to see Old Coaly then,
The Champion of the Fair.

But Coaly gladly gave us rides,
A chore he liked to do,
'Cause helping boys pretend they're men,
Why, that's important, too.

*The following is an excerpt from **Carly's Eyes**, a novel in progress. Whitney McCaine has stopped on her way home to visit a minister who has become a friend.*

THE POWER OF NOW

Faye Newman

"So you became a minister, what, to spite her?" Whitney asked.

"No. That came after I was a drug dealer and a car thief and a burger flipper. After I tried auto mechanics, motorcycle racing and running a tattoo parlor from her back porch."

"You're inventing all that."

"No. Seriously, I'm not. Wanta see my tattoos?"

"I don't know. Do I?" She smiled, searching for the rebellious youth in this poised, serene adult. Short, neatly trimmed gray hair, pale gray shirt and maroon tie, dark suit. Boyish, open face.

"Well, I'm not about to show you all of them." He stood, shrugged out of his jacket, and rolled up his sleeve. Colorful dragons breathing fire encircled his forearm, obliterating nearly all flesh color.

She burst into laughter. "Has your flock ever seen those?"

"On occasion. I haven't found concealment comforting."

"You seem, um, confident enough now."

"It took awhile, and a lot of prayers, from many different people."

"I envy you."

"I have nothing not available to you, every moment of every day."

"Uh, huh. Ri-i-ght."

"Whitney, the best thing God has given us is free will. If you're not happy, you have the freedom to make a different choice. You have the ability to choose something else, to choose to feel happy."

"You're preaching again."

"It's what I do."

"It sounds like horsefeathers to me."

He laughed. "Horses grow feathers?"

"Not literally. It's the lock of hair on their fetlocks. Um, their ankles."

"Place your feet flat on the floor. Sit comfortably, and relax. Inhale." He had a disconcerting habit of changing the subject very suddenly.

He spoke slowly, soothingly, softly. She could almost feel his vibrant voice.

"Close your eyes if you like. Breathe deeply, feel the breath all the way to your diaphragm. Relax. Feel your body relax. Let's start with your scalp. Feel all the muscles... " He continued until all the muscles in her body eased, and she sat erect but relaxed in the chair, feeling as soft as gel.

"You are love," he went on, "pure, sweet love, a thing of beauty and grace, a creature of warmth and heart. Over your head, a band of golden light seeks you out, touches your crown, and pours its power and strength into you, filling you like an empty glass, filling you to overflowing with grace and love and the power to re-create your life, now, in this moment, which is all there is. No past exists except in your memory, and no future except in your imagination. There is only the great, powerful, wondrous NOW. In this NOW, you may choose what you feel."

His voiced washed over her and through her, and warmed her and soothed her. Her eyelids fluttered and she couldn't stop them.

"What do you want to feel, Whitney?"

"Happiness," she whispered.

"And so you do. There it is, yours for the taking. It requires no one else, and no one else can hurt you. Reach out, Whitney. Take this happiness. Draw it into yourself, into your heart space, and feel it, and know it. Take it. God wants you to have it. It is yours and has always been. Take this happiness. Savor it. Taste it. Know the joy. Welcome this happiness into your heart. Take it with you. Bathe in it. Immerse yourself in it. When you go home, know that you can return to this moment, this *now* moment, and choose your joy, always. It is always there for you. Not in the future, which you imagine. Not in your past, this is a memory. In the *now*." Once more, he told her to breathe, to draw the breath deep inside her, and with it the light, and to release the light and the air and draw it back again.

Again and again, he repeated himself, until his words became part of her and seemed right to her.

She felt herself reaching out, pulling it in, bringing the happiness he said was hers deep inside herself with every breath. It *was* hers. She touched it. Sensed it. Let it seep into her corners. Lift her lips in a smile. Wondered if she was hypnotized. Wondered if she really, truly, had a choice.

And experienced, for a fleeting, joy-filled moment, flying across a fresh-cut meadow, wind whipping her hair, the sun sliding over a hill, the horse beneath her thundering, stretching, contracting, lifting, flying. For that moment, she felt the joy that had been there for her all along, that she'd left lying on the ground, untouched, unopened, alien and distant. She took it and held it and treasured it and made it hers. Her eyes filled and overflowed, and an ache tightened her throat.

At last, his voice faded to a whisper, and then stopped. He sat in silence, breathing with her. She could hear him inhale and release, inhale and release. Matched her breath to his for an unknown time.

He quietly suggested that she return her focus to the room and remember all that she had felt.

She opened her eyes. Smiled. Tears, good tears, happy tears, rolled down her cheeks.

"Thank you," she whispered. "What was that?"

He shrugged. "Meditation. Prayer. It's whatever you want it to be." His voice caressed her again.

Half in a daze, she walked across the street to her truck.

A gleaming silver scratch ran the length of its side, front fender to rear of the bed. She spun around and strode back inside to call the police.

Her anger burgeoned inside her like air filling a balloon.

"So much for choosing to be happy," she muttered.

THEOLOGY AND WELL-LOVED DOGS

Phil Hahn

I like to think that even a fairly average mind like mine can come up with a worthwhile question now and then. I particularly remember when I was about eight or nine, asking my Sunday School teacher, Sterling Melton, if dogs go to Heaven. As I recall, Mister Melton was pretty much stuck for an answer.

Since then, I've been exposed to several fairly high-powered cosmic thinkers, and so far I still don't have a solution to what I consider an important theological mystery.

Well, they say if you want something done right, do it yourself, so here goes.

It's my experience that dogs serve a high purpose in this life: they teach us lessons we need to learn. I remember a Springer Spaniel named "Squiffy," who loved to go pheasant hunting, but because of her long hair, was terribly susceptible to cockleburs. She'd spend a whole day hunting, tirelessly flushing out birds for us Great Hunters to blast away at, with no regard for her personal comfort or safety. Then, at the end of a long day, she'd be in serious pain from dozens of cockleburs imbedded in her fur clear down to her skin. It would take two of us at least an hour, with warm water, scissors, and rubbing alcohol, to dig and snip the burrs out of her sensitive undercarriage. The whole time, Squiffy would lie there, silently, patiently, waiting for us to finish. I know it hurt; she would wince now and then when we extricated one that had worked its way clear down deep and into her skin, but even then she never complained.

I guess Squiffy knew that we cared, and that we were trying our darnedest not to hurt her. And when we failed, she never blamed us. All she asked was that we do our best.

That's one thing dogs teach us, see, is that we don't have to be perfect. Regardless of what our parents may have indicated to the contrary. Dogs *always* assume that we're doing the best we can do, and no matter how pitiful our best turns out to be, they love us any old how.

There's a term for this point of view in modern psychology. It's called *Unconditional Love*. And if you can't grasp the concept, I recommend you get a dog and you'll learn it real quick.

Dogs have other lessons to teach us, too. I remember a beagle named "Henry" who got his leg broke in a fight with a car. Henry ended up with a five-pound cast on his leg, which made it difficult for him to go up and down stairs, something he did a lot. And it made it almost impossible to jump up on beds, which he loved more than life itself.

Henry wasn't home from the veterinarian ten

minutes when I heard a series of thumps, a long silence, then a few more thumps, and a humongous crash. As it turned out, the first series of thumps was Henry going up the stairs in spite of his heavy cast. The second series of thumps was Henry starting back *down* the stairs. The crash was Henry falling down the stairs. Humongously.

Henry kept this up until the cast came off. He never did master coming downstairs, but he, by God, never quit trying.

As for jumping up on the bed, I witnessed Henry's first attempt. He ran at the bed as usual, jumped, hit just about at mattress level, and fell to the floor in a heap. He then picked himself up, shook his head, and tried again, with the same result. I figured out that the extra weight of the cast had altered the aerodynamics of his beagle design, and that he could do what he was doing all day and never make it up onto that bed.

I was about to offer Henry a helping hand when he suddenly turned and clumped clear out into the hall. From there he took an extra long run, soared into the air, and landed successfully on the bed. He'd figured it out, too.

The point of all this is that Henry's broken-leg misadventures taught me not to quit just because of a little misfortune. You keep on going up and down stairs the best way you can, and you put out a little extra effort to get up on the bed or whatever. In short, you may have some problems, but you try not to let them dictate your lifestyle.

There were a lot of other dogs I learned from, but there's two in particular I'd hate to leave out. Max and Ben were two German Shepherds who, each in his own time, got old and got crippled up, as too many German Shepherds do. In their last days, they could barely walk, and some days they couldn't get up at all. In spite of this, Max and Ben would use any muscles still working to greet me at the door, tails awag and doggie kisses at the ready, as if to say "I've had kind of a bad day, but enough about me — tell me how life is going for you." Both Max and then Ben had to be put to sleep, and no dogs were ever more honestly missed or more thoroughly mourned. I wept a whole day, without stopping, for each of them, and as I write this the tears come again.

Like I said, dogs teach us unconditional love. And if we're smart, we learn the lesson and love them back. It's one of the joys of being alive.

Getting back to theology, I have to admit that I don't really know if dogs go to Heaven or not. But then, I don't really know if *people* go to Heaven, either, so I reckon it's all a matter of opinion at this stage.

All I can say is that if you describe Heaven as a place that's absolutely perfect, then by definition it has to have dogs. Because any Heaven that doesn't have a Squiffy, or a Henry, or a Max, or a Ben, has a serious flaw and really ought to be fixed.

*In this excerpt from **The Emperor's Daughter**, Julia, Caesar's daughter, laments her betrayal and exile.*

FROM THE ISLE OF PANDATARIA, 1 B.C.E.

Sandy Kretzschmar

What lies beneath the wine-dark waters of this, my solitary sea? Will the dolphins tell me? Do they hear tangled rumors from Rome; will calumny drift this far? From this wind-battered precipice I watch day and night while hollow aching fills my breast.

On the wings of morning Mare Tyrrhenum transforms, first ebbing gray, then lapping blue at midday, rolling smoky azure-green by evening and, finally, swelling purple under a midnight moon. The seasons change; the mystery remains.

If I dropped my gown on this stony shore and slipped beneath the briny surface, what would I see? Nymphs with waxen lips? Academies of mermaids? Or the goddess Venus in her chamber, receiving petitions of senatorial mermen?

Why do I still walk this barren island? What purpose do I serve? I am as vulnerable as a sea star in a tidal pool. Why am I not in the sea, transformed, pelagic, comfortable with the cold, and conspiring with Neptune to sink an imperial barge or raise a mighty storm? Why am I not frolicking with dolphins toward the Pillars of Hercules on a sunny day?

What lies beneath? Scallop-shell thrones? A procession of mermaids chosen for their virtues, sorted by the length and shimmer of their double-fin tails? Or redundant temples honoring Poseidon, like those in tribute to the gods of Rome?

What offering must I make? What can I bring to the sea?

I have not even a kithara to strum... nor a sweet voice to give praise.

I must know. This mystery of the sea engulfs me.

Grief exhausts me. My tears confront Rome, over and over, ebbing and flowing. The clamor of waves, in ceaseless droning, swallows me. My jaw tenses and my teeth grind. Were my beloved daughters used to betray me? My limbs wither without children to hold. Oh, my beautiful golden-red haired babies.

Who murdered my maid? My heart aches for dead Phoebe. Will I return home, like Odysseus? The waves roll on and on... without me.

If I were a mermaid... would I still need a mate to protect me from members of my own clan? Would I have the freedom to roam the vast oceans past Hispania? Would the Egyptian crocodile threaten me?

Could I follow the turtles of Ischia?

Or light a lamp in the night?

RISKING

Angela Lebakken

Crystal clear, icy cold water

   tumbles over rocks and sand,

      teasing me with hidden delights.

         "Take the plunge — be one with me," it invites.

         "I will refresh you, energize —

            I will inspire — fill you with

               the very essence of life," it promises.

            The icy water wins —

                  I

                    j

                     u

                       m

                         p

FIRST LEAP

Angela Lebakken

Come to the cliff, he said. They Said, we are afraid.
Come to the cliff, he said. They came.
He pushed them. And they flew.
Warrior's Wisdom by Stuart Wilde

North Dakota summer days are often hot and humid. And long. Afternoon thunderstorms cool the air, only to leave steam rising as the storm moves on and the sun blazes again. Lawns are green.

Gardens flourish with black loam bare between the rows, corn stalks tall and growing taller almost visibly; tomatoes ripen and cukes come out of hiding. The sun shines, intense, white, burning exposed patches of skin – tips of the ears, back of the neck and little slits where work gloves don't quite meet the long cotton sleeves. No breeze waves the few flowers that border the long rows. Sweat runs from the brow. The hoe and rake lay to one side of the bucket of drinking water. The dipper drips as it is raised. Mosquitoes and flies buzz and pester. There is work to be done; potato bugs to be picked off by hand, tiny weeds to chop, but clear evidence of work completed. Green, lush and rich from tender care. It is my father's garden in July, not a hobby but survival for the winter months to come in this river valley in North Dakota.

Rhubarb edges most gardens, tempting kids to swipe a cup of sugar from Mom's cupboard and sneak about, after dark, helping neighbors thin the crop. Chokecherries tell of summer's progress as they ripen along roadsides. Red juice makes tracks down my arm as I fill my bucket with fruit for Mom's jam pot. When I give in to temptation to plop the berries in my mouth I am quickly reminded why they are called *choke*cherries. I spit the acerbic juice and long for a drink of cool water.

Picking berries, garden chores and newspaper routes consume time and energy but still leave much of this child's summer days at the swimming pool in Chahinkapa Park. I take morning swimming lessons and then after peanut butter and jelly lunches I am often allowed to bike back to the pool for an afternoon of play.

At ten years old, smug and proud, I pass the test, become an advanced swimmer and am allowed in the deep end of the pool. No longer must I splash about on the shallow side or get my thrills on the water slide in the middle pool. The deep end has diving boards. Three of them. Now as I practice my dive and as I fall head first off the lowest board my mind sees perfect form and I am delighted. Splashing over to the side, crawling out of the pool with water dripping into my eyes, I look up just in time to see a friend run and jump off the high dive. It seems to take her forever to finally hit the water.

As she scrambles out of the pool to do it again, she hollers, "Come on, it's fun. Don't be chicken."

"All right, I'm coming."

The steps are cold and hard as I climb up and up. Finally, at the top, I peek down and feel dizzy. I double up my fists, plaster a gutsy smile on my face and march to the diving-off edge. Looking down again, stark terror grips me. *No, I can not jump*, my mind screams. Behind me kids are stamping their feet, muttering as they wait their turn. I am in their way but my legs are frozen to the board, toes curled under trying to get a grip.

Someone shouts, "Either go off or get out of the way."

Another kid yells, "Why don't you go back to the baby pool where you belong?" The cold, slippery steps meet my feet as, in shame and embarrassment, I retreat to solid ground. Over and over I muster courage to climb, then with head bent, I creep back down. Like the cowardly lion in the Wizard of Oz, I need magic from outside of me to make me brave.

Out of the pool, shivering and alone, I am surprised to hear Daddy call my name. How long has he been in the bleachers watching? He's never come here before. Why did he have to come now? Hot with shame I walk over to the chain-link fence that separates us.

"Angie," he says, "I'll give you this if you jump off that high dive." A fifty-cent piece rests on his palm. This is a lot of money and I want it.

Gritting my teeth, I climb up the steps again. Up, up, all the while thinking of the fifty-cent piece and the look in my daddy's eyes.

Without stopping for even a glance down or a second thought I thrust my shoulders back and walk right over the edge. I fly. I land safely with a resounding splash. Pride, satisfaction, thrill. The high dive is mine.

The high dive of long ago taught me about facing fear and doing it anyway. At the time I believed the payoff for taking a risky, non-refundable step was the fifty cents, and hard-to-come-by approval from my father. But the sheer joy of overcoming an obstacle outweighs any such rewards. I still feel terror near edges of high places where it seems like I am blindly walking into space, not knowing if and how I will land. When I do take the leap I feel the same exhilaration — angels float me to the path once more.

A NEW WORLD

Faye Newman

Fate crossed my path one day, or I hers.

I looked around and my world was new.

"Fade out," my life's Director said,

And then, "Fade in."

The sepia wash has drained away.

Nature's palette took its place.

And I'm not sure just where I am.

Where does a story start?

And where does it go from here?

Fate crossed my path one day

And all my life came new.

A TOUCH OF THE POET

Phil Hahn

I think maybe the best compliment I ever got as a writer was from none other than Muhammad Ali, the famous boxer. It was what we call high praise indeed. As I recall, his exact words were "You're not as dumb as you look, are you?"

Now that may not sound like a real spiffy compliment to you, but like they say, you had to be there.

This all happened when I was the Head Writer on The Sonny and Cher Show, and Ali had been booked as a guest. He showed up, right on time, for the first reading of the script, which he had received the night before.

As those assembled began to read through the comedy sketches, we were all amazed to discover that Ali was "reading" his script with the book closed. Nevertheless, he picked up on every cue and gave each of his lines letter-perfect, word for word. Somehow, he had managed to memorize the entire script in only one evening.

He not only knew his own lines, he knew everybody else's too. When another actor accidentally mis-read a sentence, Ali quietly gave the correct line, and then went on to deliver his own. If the significance of this accomplishment escapes you, let me say that I did TV shows for over twenty-five years, and in all that time, Muhammad Ali is the only performer who ever memorized an entire script. Much less in only one night!

But that was just the beginning. When we finished the read-through, Ali turned to me and asked if I was a writer. When I confessed I was, he smiled and said, "I write poetry." He then began to regale me with poem after poem of his own composition, recited from memory. They were terrific poems. They were funny, they were sad, they were tender, they were touching. They had rhythm and meter, and they even rhymed. Most of all, they had humor and heart. Oh, I don't suppose they would have made Lord Byron or Mister Keats worry themselves sick about the competition, but I do think they would have made Ogden Nash sit up and take notice. I have a hunch Robert Frost and Carl Sandburg might have liked them a whole lot, too.

As Ali continued, poem upon poem, several members of his entourage tried to get him to leave, but he wouldn't go. It was "Just one more," and "In a minute," until he had recited poetry for over an hour. He was obviously enjoying himself, and I suppose it didn't hurt that I was thoroughly enchanted, and told him so.

Anyway, for an hour there, he ceased to be Muhammad Ali the fighter and became Muhammad Ali the poet, sharing his work with another writer. It was a rare treat, and an honor to have been there.

Finally, Ali really *did* have to go. He got up, put on his jacket, and then he asked who had written a sketch he had particularly liked. I was pleased to be able to say I wrote it myself. His face broke into a mischievous grin, and he stuck out one of those enormous hands as he said, "Well, now... you're not as dumb as you look, are you?"

I grinned back, thanked him for the compliment, shook his hand, and Ali left. I've never seen him again, and I don't know if he'd remember me if I did. But I'll sure never forget him, nor that wonderful hour we spent in Rehearsal Hall B.

For those of you who like to argue over whether or not Muhammad Ali was the greatest Heavyweight in the history of the world, I have no wisdom and no answers, because boxing isn't my game. I'll tell you this, though: if they ever have a poetry fight and Ali is in it, do yourself a favor and bet a few bucks on the big black poet with the odd-sounding name.

RAINY DAY WALK WITH MOM

Faye Newman

I pick up Mom and Dave,
toss their bags into the trunk
and lay her walker over them.
We stop for tasty chowder in a glass café
that overlooks a naked beach in Newport
and hear the *scre-e-e* of gulls sweeping low to touch
the frothy, azure waves.
Bill arrives to check us in, we share a lovely dinner.
He knows where food is great.
Next day, we drive through Portland's seamy side,
graffiti on the walls, sidewalks growing grass,
buildings all one shade of gloom
and people's eyes just counting cracks.
Cross a bridge over Columbia Gorge
and take the north bank for this trip,
because John Kerry's here today.
The south side's glutted with fans hoping to catch
a glimpse of him sailing on the river.
The sky's turned heavy now,
and hid the sun's bright face.
Bill puts up the top a flash ahead of rain.
Though it's wet, we stop to see a mountain
jutting sheer two hundred feet above the gorge
sprouting moss on walls steep as skyscrapers.

As the shrouded sun climbs high, we reach our goal.
Alone it stands, a mansion once,
still dressed in formal gardens
its sleek green grass home to charming creatures
crafted in copper and brass.
We take time, my brothers and I, to guide our mother
up the graceful carriage drive,
around its sweeping circle to a door,
ornate and lovely; and a foyer where we pay our fee.
And then, inside, we draw a breath in unison.
Polished hardwood floors pay homage
to larger-than-life royalty and noble folks
of long ago who stand formal and stiff,
caught in the painters' talented eyes,
adorned in gowns and finery.
Queen Marie holds court before them all,
surrounded by her throne and furnishings,
each piece displaying loving care.
Upstairs, chess sets from lands afar
reside behind the glass,
Rodin graces a dozen pedestals,
a coffee shop lends rest.
In clover-leafed rooms at each end, more displays.
Native American finery holds me enthralled.
I am so glad we came!
But we're not done.
We take the long, slow walk with Mom.
We travel on, not far, to see what drew us here.
America's first memorial to the dead of war
stands lonely on a hill in Washington,
overlooking magnificent Columbia gorge.

Small Stonehenge, not carved in stone,
but poured a century past in concrete,
by a man named Sam Hill for his daughter Mary.
Attached inside each massive pillar,
the name and age of a boy,
a child, really, who lost his life in a world war.
I stand aside and watch my mother,
strong woman bent by time,
speak softly with her son,
once a wounded veteran of a later war.
I wonder what she said, the day that he came out.
It must have been the right response,
for the bond between them's only grown.
Watching them, I know
there's magic in this ancient circle.
And it has nothing to do with the altar stone.
Large enough to hold two warrior coffins
side by side,
in the circle of our mother's love.

A dream sequence from Angela's novel in progress.

ECSTASY IN FLIGHT

Angela Lebakken

Two wings of one
sleek snow-white swan
skimming the waves of a lake
so vast no shore was in sight.
Faster, faster until airborne, they soared.
Higher and higher.
The swan dropped away
as one soul touched the stars
and swung from the moon.
Venus smiled upon them,
offered a hummingbird feather
to float them gently.
Descending, they touched down
in a field of daisies. And slept.
Only to awaken and skyrocket
through the night,
a comet shooting across the night sky.
"Who are you?" Molly moaned.
The masked stranger said nothing.

COUNTRY ROADS

Phil Hahn

"Look at me!" Neva muttered, "walking down a dirt road in high heels and strapless formal with a stupid orchid pinned to my boob. How pathetic is *that!*"

The strains of the cowboy tune followed her as she trudged along the country road, outlined by the faint light of a quarter moon.

"*I-I-I love you…*" the voice twanged, "*with my whole heart… for the most part… my-y-y love.*"

"Yeah, right. That's about freaking right: 'with my whole heart, *for the most part!*' Well, that tears it for me. No more boys. Especially no more football players. No time, no how. I'll go lesbian first. Well, maybe not lesbian. What's the female for hermit?"

Neva stopped and thought it over. *Hm. 'screw or walk,' huh? And three more miles to town.* She sighed. *Well, at least he left me choices.*

She turned and strode back up the road, a grim smile turning up the corners of her mouth. She kicked a couple of rocks along the way, and giggled when she caught one just right and sailed it clear over the barbed wire fence into Elmer Thornburg's wheat field. "Three points!" she cried, raising her arms overhead in the official field goal signal.

When she reached the shiny, newly-waxed '52 Buick again, Delbert was still sitting at the wheel listening to the music, a big smug grin written across his rugged face.

"So," he remarked. "You came back."

"Yep, I came back."

"So?"

"So, the deal is, 'screw or walk,' right?"

"That's the deal."

Neva smiled. "Well, you gonna get out and open the door for a lady, or what?"

"All *right!*" the boy exclaimed, sporting an even wider grin.

As he alighted from the car, Neva pulled up her long skirt to reveal quite a lovely expanse of milky-white upper thigh.

"Like what you see, cowboy?"

"Sure do!" the quarterback replied.

"Good." Neva smiled, and kicked him in the crotch as hard as she possibly could. "Three points!" she yelled, thrusting her arms to the sky again.

As the fallen athlete lay moaning and writhing in the dirt, Neva hopped in the car and started the engine. She leaned out the window and addressed Delbert.

"You said 'screw or walk.' Well, consider yourself screwed!"

And Neva roared off down the dirt road, singing along with the radio:

"With my whole heart... for the most part... myyyy love!"

WHO'S NUDE TODAY?

Faye Newman

The Emperor has no clothes.
There he struts, exposed
in all his regal honesty.
Clarity speaks
and secrets fly.
He poses there
surrounded by courtiers
concealed in finery.
A plume sails low over a face.
A shadow screens a thought.
We search, hoping to find another
who's nude today.

BYTE ME

Phil Hahn

I think I'd like you, dear computer,
If you were just a whole lot cuter.
If you had, let's say, two breasts,
Straining in a slinky dress.
Long lean legs and toothsome thighs.
To tempt my loins and treat my eyes...
Ah then, machine, I'd love thee well,
But as it is...

   aw, go to hell.

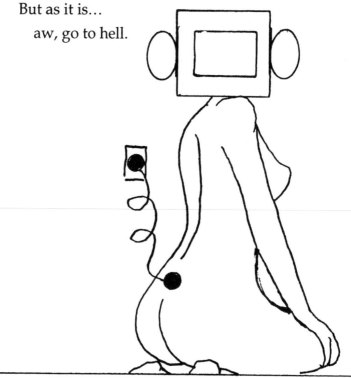

ODE TO A WRITER'S GROUP

Angela Lebakken

Perhaps we have almost gone too far
With Naked Wednesdays as our name.
Often bordering on the bizarre
One would think we have no shame.

Each individual is sane enough,
Faye, Sandy, Phil and more.
Each has humor — off the cuff,
A laugh a minute from one till four.

Put us all together, though
And the mix samples mighty strange.
We become ridiculous — a show
As we take the words to rearrange.

With love we test each written bent.
We laugh, we cry, we care
And scribble notes of encouragement
Then share and share and share.

This poem is offered all of you
A big thanks for being here with me.
No matter what I write or do
You honor my integrity.

AGING DISGRACEFULLY
Phil Hahn

I've got a birthday coming up, and I figure it is as good a time as any to try to put my life into perspective. When you get to be my age, you do peculiar things like that.

I remember this old gentleman I knew back in Kansas; we called him *Lafe,* though his full name was *Lafayette.* One day I asked him how old he was. He frowned and replied, "Old? Why, boy, I'm older than dirt."

Well, I'm not older than dirt, yet, but a little research revealed that I *am* older than TV, which probably seems pretty ancient to a lot of you. I'm also older than Rock 'n Roll, older than polio vaccine, older than HIV, older than strip malls, older than polyester, and a whole lot older than cubic zirconium. And except for polio vaccine, I could do just fine without the whole bunch.

To be more specific, I have discovered that I'm twelve years and twelve days older than Smokey Bear, I'm five years older than the Golden Gate Bridge, and six years older than Superman. On the other hand, I'm five years younger than Mickey Mouse, and the exact same age as Donald Duck.

Lest you think I'm on the verge of being a doddering coot, I hasten to point out I'm also the same age as Debbie Reynolds and Elizabeth Taylor, and they seem to be holding up pretty darn well, don't you think?

For that matter, I'm only four years older than Burt Reynolds, and only three years older than America's other great sex symbol, Woody Allen.

Best of all, I'm two years younger than Clint Eastwood and seven years younger than Paul Newman. In all honesty, though, I have to admit those last two guys look a lot better than I do, even in a dim light.

Actually, I don't believe in age. At my age, I can't afford to. I think the only important question at this stage is, have I made a success of my life, or not? Well, let's see... I *do* have a few accomplishments. I won an Emmy once, and I also caught a seven-foot sailfish, filled several inside straights, and once bid and made a grand slam in bridge. I am equally proud of all of those things.

Speaking of success, the late bandleader Guy Lombardo once said, "When I go, I'm taking New Year's Eve with me." Well, at first blush, you'd have to say he didn't succeed, because we still have it. On the other hand, New Year's Eve will never be quite the same to me without hearing Mister Lombardo and his wonderful Royal Canadians playing "Auld Lang Syne," *live*. So maybe, in a way, he *did* take it with him.

When push comes to shove, though, I'd say I personally measure success by how many days you spent on a trout stream, how many dogs you got to pet, how many girls you got to kiss, and how many sunsets you took the time to watch.

And when you consider taking things with you, it becomes pretty obvious that the money and the houses and the cars and the solid gold watches and even the Emmys you sure can't take. But I think maybe what you *can* take along when you shuffle off this mortal coil is memories of a day in the attic, a night in a tent, and the loving touch of a caring hand from someone who knows your heart. And if you can't take any of that stuff, either, then the hell with it... I'm not going.

LIFE IN A SHADOW

Faye Newman

He disappeared when he stepped into his shadow

And became it.

Cornerless carpet to places unknown,

He rode it awhile, soared aloft

Over the ashes.

Spirals of yesterdays, circle of tomorrow.

He entered his time, or another.

He never knew for sure

And spent a lifetime feeling

Lost in the shadows.

The following excerpt is taken from **The Emperor's Daughter**. *This scene takes place after Julia, Augustus Caesar's daughter, is betrayed and exiled on false charges of conspiracy and sexual scandal.*

CURSING OCTOMAN

Sandy Kretzschmar

My cries dissipate on these wild winds of Pandataria like sparks in the night from the eunuchs' fires. Therefore, I write. I imprint my curse in lead. This curse will last as long as the metal holds. Lead, the only metal I have at my disposal; I no longer have gold. The eunuchs would steal it, anyway. And, if anyone should melt the gold, this curse would be worthless, leaving Octoman with nothing to fear.

Octoman, I curse you! I curse the free life you lead.
I curse the house of Cicero and all its descendants.
May the furies wrap your dry flesh in bee stings.
May worms devour your wicked heart while you
still breathe.

You despicable nephew of Cicero! Papa should have murdered your parents as well, before you were born. You pretended friendship. You deceived me.

May your scalp grow tight, thus wrenching
your pale shifting eyes from their sockets.

Octoman, you laugh now, I know. You go about your life as usual, waddling across the senate floor, making a mockery of my name, saying, "Good riddance, Julia." Or, "Let us praise the divine Augustus for banishing his only child. Might all noble men exhibit such courage when faced with defiant daughters!"

May you soon go blind and deaf from the plague of lies you unleashed upon me.

In my mind I see you in the luxury of the baths. You are, as usual, puffed up with ostentation as you parade your pumiced and oiled body, your eyebrows, chest and armpits plucked. Falsely socializing, you recline at dice, first flattering your opponent, then rubbing your eyes as if you cannot look, feigning loss before a purloined win. In the market, while reaching for a salted sea urchin you deliberately glide your bare wrist across an ivory-skinned bosom with the pledge of true love — for an afternoon. Alas, you continue to savor your women, each the wife of an earnest man who would call you his friend.

Octoman, I curse you with the curse of financial despair, ruinous loss of reputation and total loss of self — the same damnation you have set upon me.

You devised the plan, making it appear as though I entertained five lovers at once. You bribed Thesalus to say I indulged these paramours with the pleasures of my body so they might overtake the imperium. Even now you scurry like a scabrous rat through the streets of Rome, saying you spied while I defiled the rostra. You prurient pus-filled liar. "It was an orgy like no other," you lie. "Who, but Julia, would dare to have an orgasm on the sacred rostra?"

May misery permeate your every moment.
From the pain of my heart I curse you.

My curses and incantations need a ghostly daemon to convey them across this solitary sea for a just punishment; but this isle of stones has no cemetery. Hence, I cannot lure a daemon. Therefore, I call upon Urania and her eight sisters, the blessed daughters of Jupiter.

Urania, summon the spirits of Iullus and Phoebe so they may inflict retribution.

Urania, find a daemon, one willing to embrace these leaden curses, to make them his own and to plunge them to the hilt into Octoman's fetid heart.

NOTE TO READERS:

Cursing was a common practice in ancient Rome. Some of these curses survive, written on lead sheets dredged from pools in Bath, England, or scrawled on the walls of Pompeii. Romans believed in the family patron "genius" and demon or daimon spirits. These spirits weren't considered evil until the Christian church couldn't completely dispose of the Roman pantheon and thereby reassigned demons to a more diabolical role.

OLD MEN
Phil Hahn

I remember…
Old men with white hair
Sitting in kitchen chairs
Complaining about bad backs and taxes,
Knees that don't bend right anymore.

I remember…
Old men with white hair
Recalling absent friends.
"Died in '54, no it was '55,
I remember because of the big flood that year,
Ruined the wheat,
Went up to two-fifty a bushel, that was a fortune then.
But nobody had any wheat to sell.
Rain ruined the crop. He died that year, in the fall."

I remember…
Old men with white hair
Wondering about choices they'd made.
"It was summer, in '39,
Four families just up and left their homes and farms,
The Freeborns, the Koeslings, Uncle Dee,
And what's-their-names,
Went out West to find work.
One family went to California, three to Oregon.

Wrote back they picked peaches big as softballs.
Imagine that, peaches big as softballs.
Imagine that."

I remember...
Old men with white hair
Growing out of their ears,
Remembering people they used to know...
"The Martin girl – the older one,
What was her name.
She married one of the Vandament boys,
Moved onto the old Sollner place,
Mile west of the Simon Smith Bridge,
Had a little sister who was never quite right,
What *was* her name?"

I remember...
Old men with white hair
Hanging onto life by recalling the past.
Old men with white hair
Making sure they still remembered their lives.

A HOLY ENCOUNTER

Angela Lebakken

I am fifty-eight years old and live alone. My husband of twenty-five years has moved into the city. My heart is broken open wide. It is late autumn and I remember the apples

I park my car behind the old mission church and, with sacks in hand, walk. I bend to scoot under token strands of barbed wire. Rutted tracks lead me to an abandoned orchard. The sun on my head and back warms me, eases my tense shoulders. Slight breezes refresh my skin.

As I tramp, I become aware of someone far ahead. Trudging — heavy. Glimpses as the path winds I see the person is a woman. Middle-aged, dark hair cropped short, stocky build. Is she leaving traces of her energy with every footfall? Am I picking up that subtle sense of her?

I walk — striding with care on the rocky, uneven trail. Hearing the gurgle and rush of water relaxes me. Anxiety slides to a far corner, like a jacket tossed, no longer serving a purpose. This land is high desert, water is precious. Here it gushes down from a mountain spring, tracing through a man-made wooden canal — an ancient acequia. I wonder at the design, the ingenuity of builders so long ago. It is rough-hewn but has served well for at least one hundred years. This clear water is still used by the village people — a gift from mountain gods. Certainly fairies live along this water course. Breathing in moist air nourishes both my body and mind. My shoulders slide, my knees soften and the last residue of fist disappears. The harsh world has slipped away; I have entered sacred space. I walk on. Now I am surrounded by apple trees, limbs loaded with fruit, ground covered with fallen apples.

Rounding the curve leading to the pear tree, I see her sitting on a picnic table in the tree's shade. As I approach, we make eye contact. My smile fades when I see pain – waves of pain emanating from her eyes, her heart. Her agony penetrates my chest and coats my own heart with its cloying heaviness.

"My name is Martha," she says.

"Hi, I'm Angela."

A minute, no more of chatter about deer droppings, the beautiful day. The ritual of conversation. Her voice quivers, her eyes fill and she tells me why she has come. In a voice soft with choked back tears, she says, "My son died last month. He was only seventeen — his first day of college. He sat on a railing and lost his balance. Fell two stories to his death."

Her anguish is visible. Divorced for two years, two daughters to raise, she has taken this walk with her kitten, Pearl, as her comfort and companion. She has come to sit and trace with her fingertips the initials her son had carved years ago on that picnic table.

I am quiet, present, sharing her grief. "I will pray for you."

"Thank you."

"Are you in a support group for grieving this great loss?"

"No."

"Perhaps you could find solace there."

"Yes, perhaps."

We bow our heads – an undefined moment of silence and respect. We move apart – she to go deeper into this sacred, holy place. I to pick a few apples and ponder the encounter, thankful for the gift I have been given.

THE ROCKING CHAIR
Angela Lebakken

The empty rocking chair sits on the porch in sunshine and shadow.

So often I sat in this old rocking chair. I wrote journal pages; I stared at the Piñon Pine that had become my friend. I watched jackrabbits nibble in the grass. I felt warm sunshine, dry breezes. Heard the meadowlark's song, heralding spring...

Symbolic of my leaving, it tells of emptiness once masquerading as a happy home.

The empty rocking chair reminds me of a life I lived far away, a long time ago.

NAKED WEDNESDAYS
Phil Hahn

A safe place.
To try something new.
Something weird.
Something tasteless.
To screw up.
It's okay, we love you anyway.

A safe place.
To spill your guts.
To vent.
To cry if you need to.
If life's not working out right now.
It's okay, we love you anyway.

A safe place.
To confess your foul-ups.
Goof-offs.
Failures.
Sins.
It's okay,
We love you anyway.

A safe place.
To succeed.
To be brilliant.
To be wise.
To be as wonderful
As you always dreamed
You could be.
It's okay, we love you anyway.

FA WILDFLOWER

Faye Newman

*Fa Wildflower is my lovely
Arabian mare who lost her sight to cancer.*

Fly, fly, Flower wild!
Fly across that field
To the thundering music
Of your hoofbeats.
Take my breath away,
Let my heart sing to the drums,
To the power of the life
Within your soul.

Are you truly blind?
Or is it one more illusion
To which we've all agreed?
Where have you found the courage
That lets you fly so free?
You run, as fleet of foot as ever.
I feel the breeze that lifts your mane.
I see your tail flying high.

I have to wonder, is it true?
A moment past, you couldn't see
My fingers before your eyes.
You knew me, no doubt of that.
You turned your back and spoke your ire.

"It's been too long," you said,
"Since you came to share
A moment of your time."

Ah! I see how you do it.
There behind you runs your foal,
Grown up now, she circles 'round
To cut you off,
Before you fly too far,
Before you hit that fence.
I wonder how she's earned
Your everlasting faith?

THE FAIRY

Faye Newman

I have slept
in the crook of a root
burrowed 'neath fallen leaves
with the fusty aroma
and warmth of renewal.
Wrapped snug in my
gossamer wings.

Sun's rays have found me,
warmed my nest
lit my world.
I stir
stretch my toes
breathe into them, one by one.
Peep through the leaves.
Inhale.

There a field mouse
scratches the earth
washes his face,
unhurried, skitters away.
I exhale
unfurl my wings
rub my eyes
and rise to the day.

CAROLE AND ME AND THE GRANDMA TREE

Angela Lebakken

You may be wondering, "Where is my angel?"
Your angel may be right in front of you.
Your best friend may be an angel sent to you by God.
Susan Santucci

Eagerly I sat on my front porch, in the September sun, waiting. I hadn't seen Carole for twenty years. Not wanting to waste a minute of our brief visit doing chores, I had cleaned, scrubbed and polished with enthusiasm. We would dine on enchiladas and chilli rellenos, Spanish rice and salad. Cheese shredded. Onions chopped until tears ran into the corners of my smile.

There she stood, an older Carole but with the same impish grin as if she were about to burst out laughing. Open arms met open arms in a delightful embrace. On that gentle Saturday morning, instant rapport established, I said, "Come in, come in." Talk and talk some more we did. A marathon session. Giggling at times, shaking our heads in dismay at others. She almost bounced with excitement as memories surfaced of our corny co-workers and the tricks we played long ago.

The next morning we laced up our hiking boots and set out for my favorite spot in the mountains. Pine tree scent and bird song filled the air. Leaves along the trail rustled as squirrels and unseen varmints scurried about. Purple asters flourished on the rocky hillside. Although my age, Carole's stamina and speed impressed me since I was acclimated to the 8,000 foot elevation, she was not. The steepest stretches left us both panting and halted our conversation for brief moments. Catching our breath, we leaned against an ancient alligator juniper. Much of its bark fallen away and the remaining surface weathered to a smooth grey, it stood elegantly in the sunshine. Charred scars from lightning strikes added character, like lines on an old woman's face.

"I call it the grandma tree," I said. "She must be full of wisdom from all she's seen. Oh, the stories she could tell."

We began to consider our own stories and the telling of them.

"Say," said Carole, "why don't we make a commitment to write a journal page every day for a year?"

"Okay. We'll just write a page of whatever we feel like writing."

"Yeah, but we'll exchange them, so they must be readable."

We gave ourselves two weeks at year's end to get our pages in the mail. With this commitment established, we pushed off from grandma tree and continued our trek. Since I led the way, I heard it first. Water splashing as it hit the rocks. Anticipating her surprise and pleasure, I stepped up my pace.

"What's that?"

"A spring-fed waterfall, can't you just taste it?" Rounding a bend in the trail, we arrived at the creek first and stopped, enthralled by the beauty. Shallow, still pools hosted watercress and we savored the tang of a few sprigs, as cold droplets traced down our chins.

"In April or May wild chives grow here, too. And violets bloom."

We moved on and soon came to the falls. Boulders a jumble, two stories high, formed the terrain for the creek above to come tumbling down. Silently we stood in appreciation of this wee water gift in high desert country. The path became steep and treacherous then, so we cautiously climbed until we reached the meadow: a clearing in the trees where the stream meandered before falling. We paused there, sat on a fallen log and ate the bit of lunch we'd packed. Waiting for crumbs, Piñon Jays squawked, like spoiled children demanding treats. A breeze carried the scent of dusty autumn as it blew wisps of hair across my cheek. Two trees intertwined, captured our attention and we decided they must be lovers. We crossed the creek on wobbly stones and sauntered a short distance to its headwaters.

"This is Cañoncito Springs," I said, pointing at the small, dark pool surrounded by moss-covered rocks.

"Oh, look," Carole said, "Animal droppings. Deer, I think."

With a sigh, we turned and headed back to the trail. Content and serene, my feet only lightly touched the path. A hug good-bye. The visit over. As I watched her drive away, I longed to yell, "Stop. Wait for me." I hoped our friendship would continue on a journey without destination. In the past I had scribbled journals haphazardly. This one would be different, a commitment after all. I wrote in longhand, the pen sliding over blank pages — an artist brush sensation. I made every effort at candor, soon forgetting about an audience reading these thoughts, fears, hopes and happenings. Periodically I entered the work on my computer, inserting graphics for emphasis and fun. This compilation became, "A Page a Day from Angela." Having touched a creative core, I began doing other exercises. Three pages of flow writing every morning assigned by Julia Cameron in *The Artist's Way*. Inner rooms, closed off for years, began opening their doors. My story revealing itself to me.

With pen and notebook in hand, I often trudged up the same path, sat on the same log, and recorded my page for the day. I gazed at the intertwined trees that only a few months ago had seemed a symbol of romantic love. Now, I saw those trees, not as lovers but dependent on each other to survive. As I stared and wrote I unearthed this same co-dependency in my relationship with my husband. Yearning for harmony, I was shocked to find distress and irritation appearing on the page in my handwriting. The fallen log where I rested exemplified the ominous reality that even strong entities alter over time.

As I discovered more about myself and began honoring my integrity, tensions mounted in my home. I had hiked many steep and strenuous paths with my husband. The one I traipsed now promised a new frontier, luring me inward and away from our entwined life. Sometimes I lingered near the old grandma tree, in an effort to absorb wisdom and strength. Lines, like those that gave her character, creased my face too as I groped for understanding.

Days grew shorter, nights cooler as I put the finishing touches on my year-long journal. On the appointed date I dropped the manila envelope in the mail. Suddenly I wanted those personal pages back. Like balls ping ponging in my head, my thoughts ricocheted from satisfaction to trepidation. Each day I checked the mail expecting to find her equivalent. Then, just as I had lifted the last jar of applesauce from the canner on a balmy autumn day, the phone rang and Carole's astonished voice slapped at me.

"You did it," she said. "You did it."

"What?"

"The journal pages. I got them today."

"But we said we would, we made a commitment to," I said. My face became hot and my palms sweaty. Had I misunderstood? Was I a fool?

"I know we *said* we would, but you *actually did*," she repeated. "Should I read them?"

"Well, I sent them."

"But it looks so personal."

"I don't know any other way to write a journal."

Following an uncomfortable pause she said, "Well, mine's not ready yet."

After some inane filler talk we said good bye. I stood in my kitchen looking at the phone and shaking my head. Unsure of what had just transpired, I still expected to eventually receive her daily pages. I never did.

Angry and disappointed for a time, I soon shrugged and excused her lapse. For that day in the mountains with my friend had given me the necessary push to pick up my pen and begin painting my story in strokes, sometimes bold and sometimes timid.

Carole had anchored and encouraged me during my stormy passage from shy housewife to independent woman. Then, years later, she returned to set me on my life's true path. You can overlook a lot from such a dear and inspiring friend.

MIDNIGHT SON

Betty Wetzel

Breathless, I approach his stalwart thigh.
Arched of neck, his head held high
With flowing mane and eyes so bright
Their light reflects my outstretched hand.
He's poised as if for flight
His coat of midnight blue
Glitters a most brilliant hue.
Standing aloof, daring me, daring me
To mount and show no fear.
Astride I clamber.
Ride him I must.
Forward we bound
Upward he thrusts
Up and down
Around and around
My very first ride on a merry-go-round.

MY HERO

Ina Christensen

Gramma Horn was my neighbor and my friend. She was eighty-three; I was eighteen. We would spend hours sitting on her porch talking, about anything and everything. Gramma Horn was lacking in material wealth, but was rich in gifts of the spirit.

Her worldly goods consisted of a narrow, one bedroom trailer set on a rented piece of land, her mother's brooch, assorted odds and ends of furniture, and a couple of maladjusted ducks named Henry and Henrietta.

Shortly before she died, Gramma Horn asked me if I would keep Henry and Henrietta because her family lived in the city. I agreed to take the ducks. I wanted to do something for my friend; but I also enjoyed watching the antics of the two ducks as they bickered.

Henry had to be the most hen-pecked, oops, the politically correct term would be duck-pecked fowl in existence. God help Henry if he decided to eat before Henrietta finished eating. She would swoop down and grab poor old Henry by the nape of his neck, shove his head under the water, and hold it there until she thought he'd learned his lesson. Once released, Henry would swim to shore and waddle to and fro, quacking duck curses at Henrietta.

When things got out of hand in the barnyard and Henry had had enough, he would waddle up to the house and vent to me. I would usually cluck in sympathy, then, send him on his way. Henry always embarrassed me with his cowering and giving in to Henrietta's demands. I didn't want to admit the truth. Henry's cowering behavior mirrored my own and made me uncomfortable. That was before the day Henry became my hero.

One morning I had a particularly obnoxious salesman at my door determined to sell me a set of encyclopedia that I didn't want and couldn't afford. At the time, Veneta, where I lived, was primarily a logging community. Located a few miles west of Eugene, my neighbors and I were inundated with salespeople. Among ourselves we joked about providing the training ground for beginning salespeople to learn their craft. This particular salesman was insisting that any home without a set of encyclopedia was sorely deficient.

I glanced over my shoulder at the plastic-covered windows and exposed two-by-fours of the house I lived in. He was right, it was sorely deficient. I knew a set of encyclopedia wouldn't correct the deficiency in the house or in me.

The more I protested that I couldn't pay for the books, the harder he pitched. I was too timid to go into the house and slam the door, so I stood cowering, miserable and angry with myself. Then, I heard Henry quacking.

I could see Henry heading for the house as fast as his short legs could carry him. He had an odd little habit of swinging his head side to side when he was upset. From the way he was waddling I knew he was really steamed.

After spending thirty minutes trying to get rid of a pesky salesman, I was in no mood to handle Henry's battles, too. Maybe I wasn't a match for the salesman but I could sure put a duck in his place. The minute he hit the porch I was all over him. "Don't you come whining to me, Henry!" I scolded. Old Henry just stood there and quacked, shifting his weight from foot to foot. "I don't care," I continued. "I'm tired of fighting your battles for you; it's time you learned to stick up for yourself." Out of the corner of my eye, I saw the salesman inching backwards off the porch, his nostrils flared like he had stepped into something foul. Seeing an adult conversing with a barnyard duck was more than even his tough hide could handle. Henry was still venting, but after seeing the reaction of the salesman, I didn't mind at all. The salesman scurried backwards hugging the box of encyclopedia samples to his chest like a talisman.

I heard the car door slam and told Henry to stay put while I went into the house to fetch some dried bread for him and a slice of toast for me. We sat on the porch side-by-side, toast in my hand, crumbs for Henry. It was turning out to be a great day after all.

*An excerpt from the memoir **A White Stone** by Ina Christensen*

CRACKER JACKS AND THE PRETTY LADY

Ina Christensen

In the summer, carnivals come to town. I've never been to a carnival before, but I hear the older kids talk about them. They walk around with their boxes of Cracker Jacks, and 'don't you wish you had some' grins plastered on their faces. I pretend I couldn't care less even though I do. It's not the Cracker Jacks as much as the toy hidden in the bottom of every box. Jules found a ring in his box. I really, really want a box of my own, so the next time a carnival comes to town, I decide to go even though I have no money. I know I can't buy anything, especially a box of Cracker Jacks, but I can see the lights, that's better than nothing. Like Mama always says, "Sometimes you gotta settle for what you can get." Seems to me this is one of those times. It's dark, but I'm too excited to be afraid, after all, I am nine and a quarter years old. I see the lights of the Ferris wheel. Pretty soon I hear music and know I'm going the right way.

I'm alone outside the cage where you buy your ticket. I guess this is as far as I can go without any money. I'm standing there looking at all the lights and listening to the music from the rides when a man walks up and stands beside me. He's not young like my brothers, Henry and Jules, and he's not old like my dad, either.

He's sort of in between, medium.

"What are you doing out here all alone little girl?" He has a nice smile.

I've been staring at the kids with their boxes of Cracker Jacks; I think I'm in trouble because I'm here without any money. "I'm looking at the lights."

He bends over me and gives me a friendly smile. He's nice.

"I'll bet a little girl like you would like a big box of Cracker Jacks, am I right?"

Before I have a chance to answer the nice man, I hear a woman's voice call out.

"There you are. We've been looking all over for you, you little rascal."

I don't think I've ever seen this pretty lady before, but she acts like she knows me, so I don't say anything. I think I would remember if I saw her before because she has the prettiest gold hair, that comes down to her shoulders, and the whitest teeth I've ever seen. She walks right up to me and drops to one knee. I worry that she will get her pretty dress dirty, but she doesn't seem to care. This is a very friendly place.

"I have your Cracker Jacks."

Sure enough, she hands me a box of Cracker Jacks. I see the medium age man leave real quick like. A man about the same age as the pretty lady walks up, she smiles at him and nods toward the medium aged man. I guess he's with the pretty lady.

"Take your Cracker Jacks and go straight home." She places the box in my hands, "Can you do that?" I want to tell the pretty lady, of course, I can find my way home. I got here by myself didn't I? But, that would be rude. Mama says I need to always mind my manners. I end up by nodding my head.

The pretty lady then says, "It is not a good idea for you to roam about at night. Promise me you won't do it again. Do you promise?"

I nod my head and start for home. I turn around once and the two of them are still watching. This sure is a friendly place. I sort of wish the pretty lady hadn't made me promise not to come back. But, a promise is a promise, and I'll keep mine. I hug the brightly-colored box to my chest. This is the first time I've ever had my very own box of Cracker Jacks. I'll share my Cracker Jacks with the little kids, but I'm going to keep the toy for myself. I'm hoping for a magic ring, but even if I don't get one, at least I've had my magic night.

INA CHRISTENSEN

THE NEXT TRIP TO ROME

Sandy Kretzschmar

I'm ready for you, you damn

Pygmy Gypsies.

Now I can say

Mi lasci in pace!

Leave me alone!

Out of my pockets.

Let go of my bags.

In culo alla balena!

Up a whale's ass!

Let me keep my money,

My camera and my temper.

Or I'll learn

A really good Sicilian curse.

WORDS TO LIVE BY
Phil Hahn

I'm one of those people who always tries to answer a question, whether I actually know the answer or not. I'm not sure why, exactly. Some kind of glandular thing, I suppose.

Anyway, a friend of mine recently asked me to name some of my favorite words, and I'm embarrassed to say I was stuck for an answer. The only thing that sprang to mind was the fact that, since I traffic in humor, people are forever asking me to "say something funny." My standard reply is *bellybutton*. This doesn't often lead to belly *laughs*, I admit. But it usually gets me off the hook, so *bellybutton* is definitely one of my favorite words. Besides, I don't care, *I* think it *is* funny.

According to Neil Simon in "The Sunshine Boys," the funniest words in the English language are words containing the letter "K." I happen to think he's right. Besides, who am I to mess with Doc Simon?

"Duck," for instance, is a very funny word. If you're writing a punch line, you can't go too far wrong if you end the sentence with the word "duck." Classic examples of this are "Wanna buy a duck?" and "I was *talking* to the duck!"

"Monkey" is another K-word that always leads to merriment, as in the punch line, "How about a banana for your monkey?"

(If you don't know these jokes, don't think of yourself as deprived. Think of yourself as someone who has a good laugh coming.)

But funny words aren't my only favorites. I like a lot of other words, too – mainly for one of three reasons:
1. because they sound nice to me
2. because I like what they mean, or
3. because using them makes me sound smart.

I like words like "butterfly," "eiderdown," "cannonball," and "folderol" because they "sound pleasantly to the ear," which is the definition of the word "euphonious." I like "euphonious" because using it makes me think that I sound like a person with brains.

Other words that give me the delusion of intelligence include "forfend," "mistral," "ubiquitous," and "moribund." I'd like the last one even better if it didn't mean "dying," but *c'est la vie*. (Using French words *always* makes you seem bright.)

I also kind of like "mnemonic," which means "assisting the memory," and "articulate," which means the ability to always remember the right word at the right time. I'd be *really* crazy about these two words if it weren't for the fact that I can never remember them.

One of my *very* favorite words right now is "pejorative," because I just won a bet on what it means ("disparaging," or "depreciative").

Speaking of bets, you can always pick up a few bucks in your favorite saloon by wagering on the pronunciation of the word "forte," meaning "a strength or specialty." It's pronounced just like "fort," not "for-tay," and not one person in a hundred gets it right. You might also win a few bob on "dour," a Scottish word meaning "sullen, gloomy, unyielding and obstinate." "Dour," you see, rhymes with "sewer," and not with "sour," as most people think. I personally hate to make money on that one, though, because I happen to think it would be a lot better if it *did* rhyme with "sour," and pronouncing it correctly tends to make *me* dour.

Some other words I'm inordinately (good word!) fond of are names of faraway places, like "Katmandu," "Marrakesh," "Serengheti," and "Mandalay," all of which sound so romantic you could just die. (Or at the very least, become moribund.)

All in all, though, I guess the words I like the very, very best are words whose meaning send little shivers up my spine. "Grace" and "graceful" do that for me, as do "hallowed," "joyful," "celestial," and "triumphant," to name just a few.

But the best word I know of in any language is the word "namaste," which is used in India and Nepal in place of both "hello" and "goodbye." If you listen closely in the movie "Gandhi," you'll hear the Baba-ji himself saying it quietly as he walks among his people. Not only is it the absolutely correct word for the time and place, it's a word that actually sums up the way in which that graceful little man lived his entire life.

You see, when you say "namaste" to someone, what you are saying is, "I salute God's holy light that shines from within you."

Now there's a word to live by, if I ever heard one.

AUTHORS' BIOS

Ina Christensen

Writing offers Ina a powerful form to explore her internal landscape. One such exploration led to her memoir of a painful childhood and enabled her to turn a monstrous lemon into lemonade. Foolishly, she once thought she was in charge of the creative process. Now, she knows better and listens, but writing is still the most frustrating occupation she can think of.

Phil Hahn

Phil Hahn has had 8 books published and has written over 600 television shows. He has also produced over 100 television shows. In his day he was considered one of Hollywood's best comedy writers and one of its most forgettable producers. He moved to Oregon in 1989 and took to raising rhododendrons and daughters. He's not considered an expert at either. He is currently writing a true-life saga from his checkered past, entitled, *Czech, Please — A Cold War Love Story*. So far it's going really well, and he can hardly wait to remember how it comes out.

Sandy Kretzschmar

Sandy Kretzschmar has been writing since the morning after Augustus Caesar startled her in the Vatican exhibit on Saint Valentine's Day, 1984. Although Roman art had always given her the creeps, this was bizarre. Maybe it was the full moon in Leo, the museum's sonar alarm she triggered, and the voice urging, "Someone you know is here." Whatever the cause, a writing obsession ensued. She's still writing, knowing someday she'll finish her story of learning she was once the emperor's beloved, exiled daughter.

Angela Lebakken

For years Angela Lebakken has been writing for her own amazement. She first came to *Naked Wednesdays* for help in composing an article on How to Write a Better Christmas Letter. Instead, she found herself scribbling happy little poems about the fairies and the gnomes. Then she went on to a novel that deals with time travel, love, and other aspects of the supernatural. Her ambition is to compose more startling prose and someday even write that Christmas article.

Faye Newman

When she was a kid, Faye walked to school through sheets of rain... oh, wrong tale. When she was a kid, she walked home from school telling outlandish stories to her friends to pass the time. She borrowed famous radio characters and wove convoluted mysteries, continued from day to day, around these characters. She's still telling stories and still loves it. And sometimes, they're still continued until next time.

Betty Wetzel

Betty is collaborating with her late mother on a book of reminiscences that span three centuries. Editing and polishing a treasure trove of her mother's unpublished (and previously unknown) stories of growing up in a large and loving family on a cattle ranch in a California frontier valley, Betty is intertwining her own tales of coming of age many years later, in that very same valley. Her experiences as daughter, wife, mother, grandmother, and great-grandmother serve as backdrop for her heartfelt stories of one American family.